Living Metanoia:
Finding Freedom and Fulfillment in Christ

LIVING METANOIA

FINDING FREEDOM
AND FULFILLMENT
IN CHRIST

FR. DAVE PIVONKA, TOR

Our Sunday Visitor
Huntington, Indiana

Nihil Obstat
Msgr. Michael Heintz, Ph.D.
Censor Librorum

Imprimatur
✠ Kevin C. Rhoades
Bishop of Fort Wayne-South Bend
February 25, 2021

The *Nihil Obstat* and *Imprimatur* are official declarations that a book is free from doctrinal or moral error. It is not implied that those who have granted the *Nihil Obstat* and *Imprimatur* agree with the contents, opinions, or statements expressed.

Our Sunday Visitor Publishing Division, Our Sunday Visitor, Inc., 200 Noll Plaza Huntington, IN 46750; www.osv.com; 1-800-348-2440

ISBN: 978-1-68192-552-3 (Inventory No. T2434)
1. RELIGION—Christian Life—Spiritual Growth.
2. RELIGION—Christian Life—Inspirational.
3. RELIGION—Christianity—Catholic.

eISBN: 978-1-68192-553-0
LCCN: 2021935950

Cover and interior design: Lindsey Riesen
Cover art: Adobe Stock

PRINTED IN THE UNITED STATES OF AMERICA

CONTENTS

INTRODUCTION

I'm not very good at languages. And by that, I mean I am terrible at them. It's been a family joke since the second time I took Intro to Spanish in high school. And it didn't end in high school. I can still remember sitting next to the phone in my room as a senior in college waiting for my Spanish professor to call me to let me know I passed Spanish and would be graduating. I graduated.

So, when I say I don't know Greek, I mean, I don't know Greek. But there is one word in Greek that I fell in love with the first time I heard it. I have never forgotten it, and it has been a part of the way I lived my life every day since.

Metanoia.

I was a twenty-year-old kid and was taking a year off of college serving with National Evangelization Teams (NET) Ministries. Today they call that a "gap year," but back then, we called it dropping out. One of the presenters during our training was teaching from Mark's Gospel. The very first words of Jesus in this Gospel are "The time is fulfilled, and the kingdom of God is at hand; repent, and believe in the gospel" (Mk 1:15). It is significant that this is the first thing Jesus says in Mark's Gospel. Jesus proclaims that the kingdom of God is at hand. This would have been music to

7

the ears of those listening. The Jewish people had been praying for God's reign to come, and finally the Messiah had come — the people of God would be liberated.

So, the kingdom of God is at hand. What are we supposed to do?

Repent ... in Greek, "metanoia."

In reality, the translation "repent" doesn't really do the word "metanoia" justice. It does mean repent; this is key and can't be lost. Jesus announces that God's kingdom has finally arrived, and it is necessary that we repent. We need to recognize that we have been living in a manner which is inconsistent with the kingdom of God, and we need to change. It is and will also be essential to a life of faith.

But when we look deeper into the meaning of the word, metanoia means to change, or more specifically, to change direction. We were going one way, thinking one way, behaving one way, and we need to change, to be converted.

Conversion is key, and I think it best sums up the meaning of metanoia. We all need metanoia, and there are many elements to this: repentance, change, and transformation are all integral. The other aspect that I totally appreciate is that metanoia is not a singular event. We don't really "do" metanoia; rather, we "live" metanoia. It is a way of approaching the kingdom of God, a way of following Jesus and walking toward salvation. We are not only converted once but are called to a life of conversion.

Metanoia has been my constant companion as I strive to be more like Jesus each and every day. This means continually striving to be holy, understanding this is Jesus' constant invitation. Metanoia also played a significant role in helping me live the call the Lord had on my life.

When I finished my college career at Franciscan University, which is sponsored by the Franciscan Friars of the Third Order Regular (TOR), I was fairly certain that God was calling me to be a religious priest. When I visited these friars, I learned that their primary charism was metanoia. This was one of many signs for me that this community may be my home. In my Franciscan community, we understand that metanoia is a daily, lifelong journey. Some days we do better than others, and we strive to be more faithful tomorrow than we were today. A joy of my life has been striving to live metanoia with a group of brothers who long to conform their lives to Jesus. We don't all approach this exactly the same way, and we don't do it perfectly, but we keep trying.

This is what metanoia is: continually striving for conversion so that we are more and more like Christ. This is what it means to be a follower, a disciple of Jesus.

Why Now?

I've been praying a great deal lately about the needs of the Church. We find ourselves in the midst of tremendous trials, and it seems every few weeks there is some headline or social media post about some scandalous thing that has happened. Sometimes it's about what a bishop or priest did or what some people believe he should have done. We hear stories of how many Catholics don't believe or understand basic tenets of the Faith. We argue with one another about a myriad of issues and only further divide Christ's body. I find myself getting frustrated but also realizing that there was never a perfect time in the Church. There is no such thing as a perfect time that we can go back to, if we could go back.

I think Jesus is asking something more of us, not merely that we go back to something. There is something we need today. And as I pray and watch all that's going on around us, I am convinced that what the Church needs today is saints. We need men and women who are willing to totally give their lives to Jesus, to beg the Holy Spirit to transform their lives, and to become the saints they have been created to be.

In the midst of the difficulties in the Church in the last many years, I believe at the heart of the scandal is that men and women have failed to be disciples by not responding to the call to be holy, to be saints. I then began to think and pray about what is most necessary for those of us who truly want to be a saint, and I obviously returned to metanoia. Saints need metanoia. A saint becomes a saint because they recognize their need for conversion, not because they no longer need conversion after an initial turn toward God.

Metanoia is an all-encompassing proposition. We don't simply need conversion in one area of our life, but we need conversion in the way we think, believe, behave, and love. This book deals with some of those areas. Clearly, it is not an exhaustive list, but it is one that I think begins the journey.

I hope this book invites you to examine various areas of your faith life and come to realize where you need conversion. It's important to recall that conversion is ongoing, a continual change from one thing to another. We are converted from confusion to clarity, from darkness to light, from death to life, from hate to charity — and this happens not just once in our lives, but over and over again. Conversion should always lead us to a deeper understanding of who Jesus is and who we are in relation to him. It should also lead us to be able to love our neighbor and pray for our enemies.

There are many areas where we need conversion. My prayer is that this book opens our eyes and our hearts to seek metanoia, to discover some of those areas of need in our own lives. This is just a start. I am in grave trouble the day I believe I have made it, have it all figured out, and can sit back and rest. Please, Lord, never allow me to get to that place. Always provide me the grace to continually seek to be converted to you so that I can look more like you. I pray that, as you spend time praying through this book, the Holy Spirit will show you other areas of conversion and continue to draw you closer to the Father.

Brothers and Sisters, we must live as kingdom people. His kingdom is a place where men, women, rich, poor, black, white — all people no longer live as strangers but rather as citizens of the household of God (see Eph 2:19). Each of us is called to metanoia, to be a saint, and this will look different for each one of us. When we think of the saints of the past, they are as diverse as we sinners of the present. But they embraced and were embraced by the grace of Christ and knew of their need for conversion, and so they became the saints we honor today. May we do the same.

Metanoia, the kingdom of God is at hand.

CHAPTER 1
WHO DO YOU
SAY I AM?

While I was in seminary, one of my professors constantly reminded us of this fact: "We have a Jesus-shaped God." His point was that in our discussion of God, we must start with Jesus. We don't start with some unknown supreme power, a force, or a supernatural entity; we start with a person. A person who has a face and a name: Jesus.

But who is he?

I like to imagine the scene when Jesus took his apostles to Caesarea Philippi. He was very intentional in taking them to this place. Caesarea Philippi was about twenty miles from Capernaum; it was out of the way and not really on the way to anywhere. Jesus had a very intentional purpose for taking his disciples there: Caesarea Philippi was a place of idol worship. A massive rock wall towered above a beautiful, fresh spring of water. Built into this wall were all sorts of niches containing statues of false gods. There was an image of the god Pan, the god of fertility. A large statue of

Zeus held a prominent spot. And off to the right was a massive image of the Roman emperor. To the left side of the wall there was a large cave from which freshwater flowed. The ancients believed that from this cave all life sprang forth, and the offering of sacrifices, even human sacrifices, was common.

Jesus brought his apostles here to ask them a question: "Who do people say that I am?"

Hands went up.

They had all kinds of interesting answers. "A prophet."

"Oh, oh, call on me, call on me, I know this one. Some say John the Baptist."

It seems everyone had an answer.

"But who do YOU say that I am?"

Hands went down.

Crickets.

Heads drooped, and the disciples got contemplative. Eyes closed as they pondered the mystery of the question. Peter finally looked up. "You are the Christ, the Son of the living God" (Mt 16:13–16, RSV; see also *Catechism of the Catholic Church* [hereafter CCC] 424). Yes! At least one of them gets it, at least one understands who Jesus is. Surrounded by images of false gods, the true God wants to be sure his followers understand who he really is.

Some questions are more important than others, and this one is near the top. It is a question that each and every person is going to have to answer. Who others say Jesus is can make for interesting conversation, but who you say he is has eternal consequences. We can't pass, we can't phone a friend or take a lifeline. Each of us, you and I, must answer this question. We can't just go around leaving that question "out there," unanswered.

Take a second. Who is Jesus? At this very moment, how do you answer this question? As we grow in our relationship with Jesus, our answers also change, develop, become more honest, but right now, how do you answer? Who do you say Jesus is?

Even today, the world and the crowds continue to voice opinions about Jesus. Some say he was a wise teacher or a peaceful preacher. Others see him as an agitator, the source of our culture's "problems." This is actually a pretty significant change in recent times. In the past, faith, religion, and the Church were seen as important and valuable. This is beginning to change; more and more, religion and religious people are seen as the problem. Sadly, because of the sinful things religious people have done, a growing percentage of people are looking at religion with suspicion. If a priest, who speaks for the Church and for Jesus, does something horrible, then people begin to wonder about Jesus. I recall a terribly disturbing poster a woman was carrying at the women's march in Washington, DC, which stated, "If Mary would have had an abortion, we wouldn't be in this mess." Honestly, I still pray for her, but a growing population holds this same opinion.

However, while it's important to reflect on what others are saying, in the end, what other people say doesn't matter that much. The crux of the issue is who do you say Jesus is? The Holy Father, your pastor, your spouse, or your parents and teachers may illuminate your understanding of who Jesus is, but ultimately it is you and Jesus, face to face, no ducking the question.

Who do you say he is? I invite you to think about this. A friend, a teacher, a holy man, a Savior? What are some of the images of Jesus others have presented to you? How have those impacted your image of Jesus? How has your image of Jesus changed as you have grown? Do you see Jesus the same way you did when you were twelve?

It's All in the Name

If we only look at his name, we learn something about God. Jesus is the Christ. Christ isn't his last name, rather it's a proclamation that he is the Anointed One. He is the one, and the only one, that was sent by the Father as his Anointed Son to bring salvation to the world. Jesus, as the Anointed One, brings life to the world. We are not able to come to life by our own power and goodness. We are saved because Jesus proved his love for us and died for us while we were sinners (see Rom 5:8). He rose from the dead and broke the power of sin and death in the world.

At the very moment the angel Gabriel announces the birth of Jesus, we get another hint of who he is. Jesus is the one who has come to save us (see CCC 430). Jesus came to save us because we were desperately in need of a Savior. Humanity had wandered away from God. We were eternally lost, and try as we might, we could not get back to God. Jesus comes to us and quite literally saves the day. He searches for us until he finds us and lets us know we are loved and worth looking for.

There is a great scene in one of the Superman movies where Lois Lane writes an article critical of Superman. (Big mistake.) She states that the world doesn't need a savior. Superman confronts Lois and asks her why she wrote the article. Frustrated, she yells at Superman, "The world doesn't need a savior, and neither do I." Taking Lois in his arms, Superman flies high above the New York skyline and asks Lois if she can hear anything. She can't. But he says, "I hear everything. You wrote that the world doesn't need a savior, but every day I hear the world crying out for one."

We are all in need of a Savior, and Jesus came to save the world. (Sorry, Superman, the analogy ends here.) Jesus did not come to condemn the world (see Jn 3:17), nor did he come to punish us. He did not come for the healthy (Lk 5:31), but he came for the sinner, you and me. We are the sick, the sinner. We are the ones who need to be saved. Try as we might, we can't save ourselves, we can't earn our salvation. Rather, it is a free gift won for us, paid for us at the price of Jesus' life, so that we might be saved.

There's More

Jesus, as the Second Person of the Trinity, is the Word of God (see

Jn 1:1) and the "image of the invisible God" (Col 1:15). In Jesus we are able to hear God speak. I love the reading in the Divine Office where it says John the Baptist is the voice, but Jesus is the Word.* We can hear a *voice* and not be sure what it is saying, but in Jesus, we hear the **Word**. We don't have to guess what he might say, we don't have to put words in God's mouth (but we do all the time). Jesus is the Word of God, that says everything we need to hear for a life full of hope, faith, and meaning. Jesus is the first, last, and complete Word of the Father.

In Jesus, God says it all. Jesus is the answer.

What is love? Jesus.

What is life? Jesus.

What is truth? Jesus.

What is freedom? Jesus.

What is mercy? Jesus.

What is the way? Jesus.

Certainly, we talk a lot and write a lot about what was said, but as far as a definitive word of God, it's all been said. Recall at Mass right before Communion, we all say, "Lord, I am not worthy that you should enter under my roof, but only say the Word and my soul shall be healed." What is that Word? You guessed it, the Word that is eternally spoken is Jesus, and in him we move and live and have our being (see Acts 17:28).

Jesus is also the image of the invisible God. Do you ever run into someone and they know you, but you can't quite put a name to a face? Once a friend pulled an awful prank on me. She had someone whom I had never met or seen before approach me at a conference and begin to thank me for how I had impacted her life. She went on to say how my advice and prayer was so life-changing. I was sweating buckets trying to put a name to the face. I felt horrible that I could not remember the name of this lovely

---

*Saint Augustine, Office of Readings, Third Sunday of Advent.

person in front of me. After what seemed to be forever, out of the corner of my eye I saw my friend laughing. I said to the gal in front of me, "I've never met you before in my life, have I?" She broke character and burst out in laughter. Oh sure, knock yourself out, go ahead and laugh now, for one day you will weep (see Lk 6:25).

But Jesus is the image of the invisible God, and we have a face for the name. In Jesus we discover God. God is not only Spirit, he is not just some transcendent being. But God has taken flesh and become man, and as such he reveals God to us.

This reminds me of a story about Pope Benedict XVI. The Holy Father was having a discussion with a Jewish rabbi. The rabbi was questioning what Jesus really did. He stated that we call Jesus the Prince of Peace, but we still have war; and we call him the Bread of Life, but there are still people hungry. The rabbi was questioning what Jesus really brought to the world. The Holy Father responded that Jesus brought God — he brought God to the world, and for some this wasn't enough.

What about you? Is Jesus enough for you? Saint Francis of Assisi was known to say that God was enough for him. I have prayed over this by the hour. Saint Francis didn't say that God was everything, but that he was enough. I have met people with "everything," but it wasn't enough. It's kind of a scary thing to think about, because if we say that God is enough, we are afraid that he will take everything else away from us — which, for the record, is a pretty messed up image of God. But it's a really important question: Is Jesus enough for you? Can he satisfy your heart? Is he your Savior?

Metanoia

Obviously, there is more to who Jesus is. But at some point, each of us needs to be able to answer this question: Who is Jesus?

When I was young, my image of God was basically this: If we were bad, he was going to punish us. If something went wrong, it must be because I or someone did something wrong. Now before you think how silly that sounds, and I know it does, I am not alone. Look at John chapter 9, when Jesus is asked whose fault it is that the young man was born blind. They assumed blindness was a punishment from God for sins committed by the young man himself, or by his parents. It wasn't until I was about twenty years old that the Lord broke into my mind and heart and said to me, "Dave, that's not the kind of God I am." Those words changed my life and my image of God, and over the last many years, I have heard God say this to me countless times. My prayer is that you hear this as well. What's your image of God that needs to change?

Jesus reveals to us who God is. I don't know if anyone has a perfect image of God; we all have room for conversion. I heard it said once that we were created in God's image and then we returned the favor. We tend to make God out to be who we want him to be — a God who supports all of our causes, our recreation, and our political views. We want a loving, merciful, patient God for us, but we want "those people" punished. We want a God of freedom, but then we get upset when he challenges how we use our freedom. We want the grace or "benefits" of all that God offers without him asking any kind of personal response of us. I remember a young woman sharing with me some elements of her life that were clearly sinful. She went on to say that because she "enjoyed" it so much, she could not imagine a God who would not let her continue this behavior. I invited her to do just that: to imagine a God who was possibly asking her to change.

We like to have God figured out. The thought of our image of God changing, developing, and growing can be a scary proposition. But so is the alternative. The thought that I have God totally figured out, that I have no more need for conversion, growth, or understanding, is, to me, even more frightening. To think that I, Dave Pivonka, finite, wounded, and sinful, have the almighty, omnipotent, all-holy God totally figured out is simply laughable.

I — we — need our minds to change regarding our understanding of God.

A significant moment of conversion for us is when we can surrender the images of God that we have created and seek to have God show us who he really is. It's a step in faith, and at times kind of scary, but it's necessary if we are going to grow and develop in our walk with Jesus.

Take some time and ask the Holy Spirit to bring to you images of God you have that are not correct. Spend some time reading one of the Gospels and let Jesus shape your image of who God is. Pray that God will move you from your limited image of who he is to who God really is. Sit and contemplate how you answer the question, "Who do you say that I am?"

Questions

How would you describe your relationship with Jesus to a friend?

How have you seen your understanding of who Jesus is change as you have grown in the spiritual life?

What is one point from this chapter that caused you to look at God, yourself, or others differently?

Metanoia Moment

Come, Holy Spirit.

The saints spoke of Jesus in many varied ways, but he was Lord to all of them. Take a moment and ask Jesus to place on your heart the same Spirit that moved Saint Peter to proclaim Jesus as the Christ — the same Spirit that moved all the saints to conversion. Pray for the grace to see Jesus as he is and to fully give your heart to him.

CHAPTER 2

WHAT MUST I DO TO INHERIT ETERNAL LIFE?

Some questions are more important than others. I suppose asking and being asked questions is part of life, but seriously, some questions are just more important. "Do you want more chips and salsa?" This question doesn't have much cosmic significance. And yet, there are questions of greater importance. Just ask any guy who's gotten down on one knee, nervous and sweating, and popped the big question: "Will you marry me?" While I don't know from personal experience, I can imagine that, for a moment, the world stops spinning. The answer to *this* question may very well change the direction for many people's lives.

It's obvious that some questions are small and relatively insignificant (more salsa?) while others are more monumental: more chips? But, I want to suggest that there is one question that is more important than all others.

"What must I do in order to get to heaven?"

I propose that this might be the most important question any person will ever ask. This question is infinitely important. Can you answer this question? I'm afraid too many Catholics simply don't know the answer to this most fundamental question. When I ask people what they think they need to do to get to heaven, I get all kinds of answers. People talk about going to Mass, tithing, not hurting others, praying the Rosary, and being nice. I get it, I mean, it's nice to be nice. But we don't get to heaven just by being nice, by not being mean, or by saying prayers before dinner. Obviously the Rosary and Mass are vitally important to our spiritual life. But is that it? If our eternal life gift card has all the appropriate holes punched, are we good to go? Is that all we need in order to gain entrance to heaven?

Over the years I have asked many, many Catholics what we must do in order to get to heaven, and I have received answers similar to the ones previously mentioned. Rarely, however, do individuals mention Jesus. I want to be absolutely, 100 percent clear: We don't get into heaven without Jesus. Jesus is THE Way to get there!

Running to Jesus

Jesus had been in Jericho for a couple of days and was about to leave the city when a rich young man ran up to him. "I have to ask him a question before he leaves!" So the young man runs to Jesus with a question burning on his heart.

He asks Jesus, "What must I do to inherit eternal life?" (Mk 10:17). I love this image of this brash, rich kid in front of a simple carpenter asking what he needs to do to get to heaven.

This young man is bold in approaching Jesus, but it's essential that he asks this question. There is something different about Jesus: the way he treats people and how he speaks. The young man believes that Jesus knows the answer to his question.

Do you know? I mean, do you know what YOU must do to

inherit eternal life? Can you answer this without hesitation? With 100 percent certainty? If you don't know, you must figure this out before the sun goes down today. There can't be any fuzziness or confusion. What do we need to do in order to get to heaven? There is no need to be afraid or worry — the answer is right before you, but you need to know this answer.

Are the Commandments Still an Issue?

Jesus' greatest desire is that you and I get to heaven. He wants the rich young man to get to heaven even more than the young man does. When asked about heaven, Jesus starts by telling the young man to keep the commandments.

I love Matthew's version of this story; the young man responds, "Which?" (Mt 19:18). I find that pretty funny and so familiar. When I was teaching, I would so often get asked, "What do I need to study for the test?" (I don't want to learn anything more than I absolutely have to!)

But what a question: Which commandments are the really important ones? I mean, the first commandment seems non-negotiable, but if I do a good job with it, can I get an occasional pass on the third? Is the tenth commandment optional if your neighbor has extra-cool stuff?

Or maybe it's about percentages? In most classes 70 percent is passing, is that how it works? Clearly 50 percent on the commandment scale isn't going to cut it, but maybe God will grade on a curve because I am a lot better than Molly down the street.

Here's the thing: The commandments matter. All of them. I once heard a story about a hotel manager near a college campus. One night he was working at the front desk, and two students showed up asking for a room. It was clear to this manager that the two were not married, and he told them that it wasn't right for them to get a room together. (Obviously, this happened a long time ago. I can't imagine many hotel managers asking this question any more.) The kids retorted, "Oh, it's OK, that command-ment isn't such a big deal anymore." The manager was shocked at the news and called his pastor to check. He was relieved to hear that yes, there are still ten commandments.

But it is really important for us to understand that the first thing Jesus says to the young man is to follow the commandments. We can't look at the commandments as outdated, archaic, and ir-relevant. The commandments are still vital, and for those inter-ested in everlasting life, they will always be essential. For all ages, times, purposes, and circumstances, the commandments matter. Public opinion polls and cultural trends don't change objective re-alities. Some behaviors have been and will always be sinful. I know this is terribly counter-cultural, but it's true.

The commandments matter, and they mattered to Jesus. In fact, Jesus raises the bar on the commandments. He talks about the commandments being written on our hearts, not just remain-ing as external laws. The commandments tell us not to commit adultery, but Jesus tells us that "everyone who looks at a woman lustfully has already committed adultery with her in his heart" (Mt 5:28). The commandments tell us not to kill, but Jesus tells us not to even harbor anger (see Mt 5:22). Jesus doesn't just want us to avoid evil, he wants us to love one another "as I have loved you" (Jn 13:34). Things change once Jesus comes on the scene.

At first glance, it may seem like Jesus makes the command-ments more difficult. However, he also provides us all the grace to be able to follow the commandments. More on that later.

Back to the rich young man.

Hearing that he must follow the commandments, the young man is feeling pretty good. The rich young man replies to Jesus, "Teacher, all these I have observed from my youth" (Mk 10:20). That's a bold statement. Who of us can say that? I've followed all the commandments? He must have been shocked to hear that there was still more. Eternal life is about much more than just following the law.

The commandments matter, but they are not the only thing. We can't earn our way to heaven just by not doing bad things. Heaven isn't a ticket that can be punched; it's not about having a positive balance sheet or a good report card. Never skipping my prayers doesn't win me eternal life. A "holier than thou" attitude doesn't cut it. After all, the Pharisees followed the commandments to the letter, but Jesus was most critical of them. We can't just act our way into heaven.

The One Thing

After the young man says he has kept all the commandments, Jesus looks on him with love (see Mk 10:21). This is such a beautiful and important line. Nothing really makes sense apart from this. Jesus looks on him with love. We need to keep this in mind: Everything Jesus ever says or asks of us is always in the light of his love. It is imperative that we understand this.

Jesus, having looked at him with love, replies, "You lack one thing" (Mk 10:21).

At this point the rich young man must be feeling pretty good and excited.

Are you serious? Just one thing? That's awesome! I'm even better than I thought!

But this *one thing* presents a challenge for the young man. Jesus tells him, "Go, sell what you have and give to the poor, and you will have treasure in heaven; and come, follow me" (Mk 10:21–22). For Jesus, eternal life is not just about following the commandments. To gain eternal life we need to be able to get rid of whatever keeps us from following Christ.

What's Your Thing?

It's important to bear in mind that Jesus is not saying the way for *everyone* to get to heaven is to "sell what you have and give to the poor." It's clear that possessions are what kept *this* young man from following Jesus. Before he was free to follow Jesus, the rich young man needed to rid himself of the things that kept him from totally following Jesus. For this young man, it was his riches. For others it is fear, insecurity, anxiety, control, selfishness, pleasure, reputation, or certain relationships. Other people feel they can't follow Jesus because of their addictions, sins, or past mistakes. There are all kinds of things that prevent us from following Christ. The question we must answer is what is Jesus asking of us? What is he asking of you? What's keeping *you* from saying "yes" to Jesus right now? What must we get rid of in order to follow him?

In the end, I find this story to be incredibly sad. The young man wants to inherit eternal life, he is faithful to the commandments, but in the end, he walks away from Jesus, from the Way to eternal life. Jesus knew this young man's things were going to keep him from gaining eternal life, and because he loved the young man so much, Jesus asked him to let it all go. He didn't want the young man to have anything keeping him from eternal life. Still, Jesus loves and respects this young man and his freedom so much that he won't force him to do anything. Jesus wants him to give freely. But the young man chooses his things instead of Jesus and walks away. The young man is sad because he can't give to Jesus what is being asked.

A Scary Story

This story is sad, but it's also a bit scary once we realize that Jesus asks us to sacrifice as well. Jesus asks you and me to give up whatever is going to keep us away from him. This is our metanoia moment. Although it will often be very difficult to surrender, it is a great moment in our conversion when we take this step in faith and pray, "Lord, take whatever keeps me from you." Take a moment and pray for that again. "Lord, I surrender whatever keeps me from you. Allow me to see what that is and take it from me."

I understand that this can be a frightening prayer. It's one of those prayers that puts our faith in perspective and brings clarity. Ask yourself: Am I able to say, "Jesus, take *whatever* keeps me from you"?

I experienced this moment of stripping away a number of years ago, the night before I walked the Camino de Santiago, a five-hundred-mile pilgrimage in Europe. The evening before I began my walk, I was praying in a small, beautiful Gothic chapel. I felt my heart pulled to leave behind whatever was keeping me from Jesus. I remember praying, "Jesus, I give you everything. I give you permission to do whatever you want to make me holy." I must admit there was a bit of trepidation in the prayer. What might he do? What would he ask of me? What would I need to surrender?

While this can be a bit scary, it is also liberating. It's an act of trust and surrender that frees us to follow God more closely. It's Peter getting out of the boat and walking on the water. It's us saying to Jesus, "This is scary, but I know you will take care of me. I trust in you." The liberation we experience from this surrender is more beautiful and fulfilling than the things that keep us from God in the first place. Imagine being free from whatever keeps you from God!

Jesus asked the young man to give up his possessions, but this isn't necessarily what he's asking us. We need to figure out what Jesus is asking us to surrender. What are you holding on to? Right now, what do you treasure more than being in relationship with Christ? Keep in mind that the young man didn't ask himself this question, he asked Jesus. And so must we.

The Narrow Gate and the Way

Maybe it's a paradox. It seems that getting to heaven is both extremely easy and profoundly difficult. If we want to get to heaven, we need to follow Christ and follow the commandments. In 1 John it says that if we love Jesus, we will keep the commandments (see 5:3). So, that doesn't seem so difficult. But Jesus also says that the road that leads to heaven is difficult. He says it's a narrow gate, a narrow road. Having grown up in Colorado, I've had the opportunity to hike on paths that are perilous. It was essential that I paid attention to where I was walking, or I could have fallen and been hurt. Jesus invites us on this type of path — a path where we don't know the way, where we must be careful and pay attention or else we may get in serious trouble. Staying on the road that leads to life demands attentiveness and intentionality. There will be all kinds of roadblocks and detours along the way, but if we pay attention and keep our eyes and heart on the Lord, we will be fine.

To be clear, we don't just happen upon this path; we must choose it, daily, and decide to continue on the way. Some days will be more difficult than others, but we keep pressing on, we run the race, keeping our eyes on the prize.

So, what are you holding on to right now that keeps you from the Way of Jesus? Is it your own will? Your fear? Is it that you are anxious about what he may ask of you? Maybe you have anxiety about how your friends, family, or peers might react. Is it your past? Your future? Perhaps you don't want to change something in your life, or you are afraid you can't change. Maybe it's your money, possessions, and security? Maybe it's even your sin? There are many things that we feel can keep us from saying yes to Jesus, but we need to be absolutely clear about this: The only reason Jesus is asking them of us is because they are what keeps us from him. That's it. He's not mean, controlling, or needy. He doesn't want to take your hopes and dreams. All he wants is the thing that keeps you from him. He wants us to give him whatever may keep us apart from him for all eternity. Don't forget that ultimately what is at play is our eternity. Jesus has prepared a place for each of us;

he knows the way. Let us follow him so that one day we may reign with him.

Questions

How would you explain to a friend how a person gets to heaven?

Jesus looks at you with love and then asks for whatever keeps you away from him. What does he ask of you?

Metanoia Moment

Come, Holy Spirit.

Saints are those who get up one more time than they fall. Our decision to follow Jesus is a constant choice, one that we make time and time again. Take a few minutes and consider what God has done for you, how he has loved you, how he has been patient, kind, and merciful. Once again, give your heart to the Lord and choose to follow him on the road to eternal life.

CHAPTER 3
DEATH AND LIFE

I enjoy adventures. I love to take trips where I have a basic plan of what I will be doing, but there are enough unknowns that it makes it interesting and exciting. I had such an experience with some friends of mine when we went to Peru and spent three days hiking what ultimately took us to Machu Picchu, the ancient ruins of the Mayans. While there was planning done, most of it was done by my friend, and there were many instances where we did not know what to expect — which I am OK with, to a point.

There were the little surprises, things like the food we would eat on a given night. I must be honest and say I wasn't thrilled with the local delicacy of guinea pig but was willing to try it, along with alpaca. Neither of them was great (actually one was awful), but it was a part of the adventure.

Our hike took us through the Peruvian Andes and ultimately to 14,800 feet, but I like to round up to 20,000. The views of the Andes Mountains were breathtaking, but it was really hard work. There was a price to be paid for such views: It was a hard hike. I mean really hard. My body wasn't accustomed to exerting effort at that elevation, and it was yelling, "Give me oxygen!" Every few minutes I would have to stop and try to catch my breath. Those three days were probably in the top five most strenuous, physically challenging days I had ever done. It was really difficult, but I wouldn't trade it for the world. It was a wonderfully thrilling adventure.

And Machu Picchu was all I had hoped for. It was such an amazing experience to see something in person that I'd seen so many times in photos and on TV. Machu Picchu is so fascinating. In this small space there are over 150 buildings and more than one hundred different flights of stairs. It's believed that the thousands of stone blocks used in the construction, most being over fifty pounds, were pushed and carried by the Incas, who did not use any kind of wheels. And I thought my hike was difficult! The construction is so precise and the cut stone so perfect that a knife blade does not fit between the stones. The location is stunning with the rich green mountainside. It was an "I can't believe I'm here" moment.

A Greater Adventure

As great an adventure as it was, it was not my greatest adventure. Nothing compares to my journey of faith, my walk with Christ. To follow Jesus, to walk with him, is the adventure par excellence. It's one filled with twists and turns, valleys and hills, highs and lows that we never expect. There are times of tremendous happiness, such as the day I was ordained a priest. I can't explain the joy I experienced that day. My family and friends were all present to celebrate with me. It was such a grace to kneel before the bishop and have him lay his hands on my head and pray for the Holy Spirit to anoint me a priest. It was also moving to have my brother Franciscans lay hands on me as well, praying the Lord's blessing. It was such a moment that even reflecting on it today moves my heart.

There have also been times of heartbreaking sorrow. To be with friends who are forced to deal with the loss of a loved one is so difficult. And at the same time, when grace is a part of that experience, it can also be beautiful. It's hard to imagine that suffering and pain can be beautiful, unless of course you have experienced it — if you know, you know. This is one of the mysteries of our faith.

In our walk of faith, we don't know exactly what is going to happen and where we will be led. There are enough unknowns to make it interesting, but Jesus does give us some insights into the journey.

And one thing Jesus is absolutely clear about: It's going to be difficult, and this should come as no surprise. Life is difficult; it just is. Following Christ doesn't make the circumstances of life any less difficult, but Christ can take those same difficulties and make them transformative. To live a life striving to be faithful to God, seeking holiness and heaven, is going to be tough, and Jesus reminds us that the cross is central to this journey. Over time I have discovered that Jesus' cross is both terrifying and liberating. However, it has become the companion that keeps me firm on my journey of faith.

Deny Yourself and Pick Up Your Cross

The cross is at the heart of Jesus' conditions for discipleship. He tells that us if we want to follow him, we must deny ourselves and pick up our cross. It's remarkable that Jesus decides to lead with this. I just don't think it's the best marketing plan if you want to attract followers.

The glossy pamphlets marketing my trek in Peru said nothing about blisters, difficulty breathing, people needing oxygen, knee problems, and headaches from altitude sickness. What they did have were lots of lovely, sun-drenched photos of mountains, fields of wildflowers, waterfalls, and the palace of Machu Picchu — all used to entice the consumer into the trip.

You must love how honest Jesus is. He doesn't lead with the joys of the beatific vision but with what we are going to go through before we get there. If I was marketing something, I'd be sure to lead with the good stuff: "New triple-stuffed Oreos, more of what makes them delicious" sounds a lot better than "New triple-stuffed Oreos, sure to put ten pounds on you by Monday."

But Jesus isn't afraid to lead with hard truths. He doesn't pull a bait and switch. He wants his followers to know what they're getting into because he wants his mission to be fully embraced. Life in Christ is not easy. However, Jesus does promise us that it will be worth the effort.

To Live, We Must Die and Deny

The very first thing Jesus invites us to if we want to follow him is often very difficult. It is part of the cross: We must deny ourselves. Think about this for a moment because this is important. Jesus is saying to you and me that if we want to be his disciples, if we want to be his followers, we must deny ourselves.

For many Catholics this comes as a surprise, and more often than not, self-denial is not at the top of our "to do" list. However, we need to reconcile this apparent discrepancy. If we want to follow Jesus, we must live a life of self-denial.

Do we?

Do you?

Do you live a life of self-denial?

Is fasting a part of your spiritual life (not only in Lent, but at other times of the year)? Is it a regular practice in your life and the life of your family? Other than when the Church says we must, do we abstain? How often do we go without? Do we surrender our will for the will of another? Do we say no to our flesh and its cravings?

I get it — this is difficult. We want things, our flesh has cravings while seeking ease and comfort. It's difficult to say no to ourselves. However, there is something central about being a Christian that invites us to sacrifice, to deny ourselves. Padre Pio often spoke of this, stating that much of the spiritual life is a battle in learning to die to ourselves.

We most often associate self-denial with fasting, and this is a part of it, but it's more than that. Part of self-denial is saying no to things that are opposed to the kingdom of God. It is saying no to the temptations of sin. Obviously, this is key, but saying no to sin is like saying no to putting your hand in the middle of a campfire. It's not something we should ever be doing, so we shouldn't need to say no to it.

I recall talking with a young man who was experiencing a deeper conversion in his life, and he was sharing with me what he was going to do for Lent.

"I am not going to get drunk or high and will stop having sex with my girlfriend," he told me.

Now, those are really wonderful things, but I suggested that he extend his forbearance beyond Lent. We should constantly be saying no to sin and temptation. But as everyone knows, this is often difficult. And this is where our saying no to other things helps us. If we can get in the habit of denying ourselves smaller things, and in doing so gain mastery over ourselves, we grow in our ability to say no to sinful things. There is an absolute, total connection between our ability to deny ourselves and our ability to say no to sin, to temptation, and even to our addictions.

Self-denial is not only directed toward temptation or things that are sinful. We are invited to deny ourselves things that may be morally neutral or even good, but to do this for a greater good. Sweets are a good example. There is nothing wrong with me having a dessert, but saying no to it might help me to grow in the virtues of discipline and self-control.

If I am being honest, when I think back to most of the stupid things I have done in my life (and there are many), at the root of most of them was an inability to deny myself. My lack of self-control, procrastination, over-indulgence, speech, impatience, pride are all rooted in an inability to deny myself. It's pretty simple: If I were better at denying myself, I would sin less.

We live in a world of utter extravagance, a world where more is better and most is best. Advertising agencies and the evil one use the same tactic: "You want this, and you should have it." It was the tactic of the serpent in the Garden of Eden and continues to be his way of attacking us. Given that the world and the evil one are trying to feed our expansive appetite, it's no wonder that fasting and abstinence are difficult. We've moved away from self-denial into a world of uber-options. In this world, fasting and abstinence seem almost archaic.

Yet just a few decades ago, fasting and abstaining were a central part of a Catholic's life. Catholics wouldn't even think about eating meat on Friday. There were so many Catholics abstaining from meat that businesses had to adjust. Why do you think McDonald's came up with the Filet-O-Fish? The chain wanted a way to sell to Catholics even on Fridays and during Lent. Never underestimate McDonald's' desire to sell something to us.

Here is something that might take you by surprise. The Church still asks Catholics to abstain from meat (or some other food) every Friday, not just during Lent (see *Code of Canon Law* 1250–51). Fridays are to be days of penance and should be marked with some type of fasting. Canon law also gives bishops the ability to determine some other type of penance, which is the case in the United States, but the truth is that the vast majority of Catholics do not practice any fast, abstinence, or act of penance on Fridays. This is unfortunate for a couple of reasons. First, these are practices that God is inviting us to do, and second, they are a part of our Catholic identity.

I believe we would do well to spend some time reflecting on fasting. Saint Anthony of the Desert believed this to be central to the spiritual life, preaching that if we want to grow in the spiritual life, we must learn to control our stomach and tongue. We can't be slaves to food or comfort. As a side note, Saint Anthony also believed we need to be able to control our tongue by how we speak. Fasting from speaking is often a very powerful practice.

Now, there is a delicate tension here. Hearing that we are supposed to deny ourselves can lead some to believe that God never wants us to have good things. This isn't the case. There is nothing wrong with having ice cream, chocolate, or a glass of wine. There is something wrong if we can *never* or will never say no to those or other things. And to be clear, it's not just about the "no" but about what our ability to say no does for our spiritual life. I am under no illusion that my fasting is going to change the world, but it might change me. If I can say no to ice cream, alcohol, or meat on Friday, taking the elevator, or speaking negatively, then maybe I will grow in self-control. Then the next time I am tempted to do or say something, I will have grown in my ability to resist.

It must be noted that self-denial is not about saying no just to say no. Our faith is not ultimately about a bunch of "no's" but our ability to say yes. I am not merely encouraging you to say no to some things to make you depressed and miserable. On the contrary, my prayer is that saying no actually moves your heart to be able to say a greater yes to Jesus.

There is something powerful in this desire to grow in mastery of our flesh. Just because our body or mind may want something does not mean we have to say yes. It is okay to say no — or even just to say "wait" — to yourself. In one of his letters, Saint Paul talks about treating his body hard and making it obey him (see 1 Cor 9:27). This doesn't mean you have to totally neglect yourself; instead, it is a reminder to put everything in its place. Your body is important, and enjoying the good things of the world is important, but your soul is the most important thing of all. Food, sleep, physical intimacy, and other things are all powerful desires. But these desires shouldn't control us, we should control them. There is an intimate and necessary connection between our ability to deny ourselves and our ability to follow Jesus more closely. There is an intimate bond between denial and picking up our cross. Denial must come before the cross. It's a prerequisite. We won't have the strength to carry our crosses if that strength doesn't spring from our ability to deny ourselves, to do hard things for love of God. If we can't learn to deny ourselves in different ways, we won't be able to be faithful to the second condition of discipleship: picking up our cross.

This Is Difficult

Life is difficult. Life is also wonderful, but as wonderful as it may be, it is still difficult. There is no escaping that at one time or another, everyone is going to experience hardship, burdens, suffering, and the cross.

Jesus asks — commands — if we want to be disciples, we must pick up our cross. We can't take this as some poetic, saccharine, or sentimental statement. The cross is real; it's difficult, and nothing about it is easy. Who hasn't struggled with their cross or asked why it had to be this way? Who hasn't asked Jesus to take their cross away at some point in their life? We have all had these "agony in the garden moments" throughout our lives.

A friend of mine who had cancer would always say that it was her cross. She continually prayed that Jesus would take it away but knew that it was not up to her whether or not she would be healed. What was up to her was if she was going to embrace the cross, to accept the Father's will and encounter God in the midst of her agony in the garden.

It is not being a Christian that brings us difficulties; rather, it is being human. Suffering, pain, sorrow, fear, abandonment, and loneliness are not merely Christian experiences — they are human realities. However, Christians can see all of these realities transformed and graced.

I once knew an elderly professor named Grace who was dying. She was suffering a great deal and was constantly going in and out of consciousness. Even though she was in pain and it was clear that she didn't have much longer to live, she kept saying, "No, not yet. I want to be with Jesus, but I want to suffer with him a little longer." Grace had discovered the mysterious grace that is present in suffering: union with Jesus. I realize that this is an extreme example, but Grace was experiencing union with God that was transforming her. Rather than running from suffering, she was embracing it and praying that she could suffer just a little longer to be able to conform her cross to Jesus. I believe that is supernatural.

This truth is so vitally important to our spiritual life. It's probably one of the most important points but often least understood or experienced. If we can find Christ, and ultimately, joy, peace, and love amid the cross, then we can find him anywhere. It's easy to find God in the joy of a wedding, the birth of a child, or a baptism. But something changes in us, an experience of metanoia, when we can find him in broken relationships, in dementia or in cancer, in loss or in infertility. When we can find Jesus in these dark places, well, we have few dark places because he always shatters the darkness with his light. Hope becomes our reality and our experience, not just something that we wish for.

Jesus desires to reveal himself in these messy, hard, and painful situations. He often doesn't take them away, but we can experience his comfort, his healing, his presence, and his light in the midst of darkness. He is in your pain, your fear, your regret and confusion. Ask Jesus to show himself. Like the persistent widow, keep praying, asking Jesus to make himself known in your difficulty.

We Can

We don't have to do this alone.

I love the story in Mark's Gospel where James and John ask Jesus if they can sit on his right and left in heaven. In response,

Jesus asks them: "Are you able to drink the chalice that I drink?" They respond confidently, "We are able" (Mk 10:38–39). I love that they say "we are" rather than "I am." By ourselves suffering is so much more difficult, and it is so hard to persevere, but together we can. Because we are in the Church together, we do not have to approach our crosses by ourselves. We don't do hard things alone; we do them together.

When I was hiking the Camino, I met an elderly couple who was making the trek for the second time. That in itself is amazing. People often ask me if I will walk it a second time. NO! It was a wonderful experience ... once. But the most remarkable thing about this couple was that the gentleman was blind. It was profoundly moving to watch this elderly couple walk. The husband would place his right hand on his wife's left shoulder, and they would walk together. There is no way he could have completed his journey alone, but together they could.

This is central to the spiritual life: We walk it together as brothers and sisters in Christ. We walk it with Jesus leading the way. We walk, and at times it is hard and painful and scary, but we don't walk alone. There is something beautiful, something holy, when we are invited to walk in another person's suffering. Suffering is so personal and intimate, but when we open our heart to another, we invite them into our brokenness, and this is sacred. There is something holy in this vulnerability. I think this is revealed to us with Jesus on the cross, beaten, naked, and exposed for all the world to see. He does not hide his brokenness but invites us into it. It is graced, and this grace allows us to keep pursuing Jesus, knowing we are not alone and do not have to give up.

Saint Josemaría Escrivá says, "Jesus did not say you would not be troubled, you would not be distressed, but He did say you would not be overcome."* The Christian call to take up our cross

---

* Josemaría Escrivá, *Christ Is Passing By*.

is daunting, but we already know the ending, and it's a good one.

Being a disciple is difficult. It continually makes demands on me and my life. It invites me to be humble, to be a servant, to surrender, to go without, to die, and I would have it no other way. My life of discipleship has been filled with purpose, with meaning. I believe it has also been a blessing to others and has, I hope, given witness to the goodness and the beauty of God.

Questions
The paradox of the Christian life is that "in order to live, we must die." How have you experienced this death to self?

As a Christian, how have you experienced the call to be counter-cultural?

What are two practical ways that you can practice self-denial?

Metanoia Moment
Come, Holy Spirit.

Take a moment to think about some of the difficulties and crosses in your life. If you are able, ask for the grace to accept this cross. Pray for the grace to see God in the midst of the difficulty and ask Jesus to be with you and strengthen you as you carry this cross for love of him.

CHAPTER 4
SIN AND MERCY

One of the Pharisees asked him to eat with him, and he went into the Pharisee's house, and sat at table. And behold, a woman of the city, who was a sinner, when she learned that he was sitting at table in the Pharisee's house, brought an alabaster flask of ointment, and standing behind him at his feet, weeping, she began to wet his feet with her tears, and wiped them with the hair of her head, and kissed his feet, and anointed them with the ointment. Now when the Pharisee who had invited him saw it, he said to himself, "If this man were a prophet, he would know who and what sort of woman this is who is touching him, for she is a sinner." Jesus answering said to him, "Simon, I have something to say to you." And he answered, "What is it, Teacher?" "A certain creditor had two debtors; one owed five hundred denarii, and the other fifty. When they could not pay, he forgave them both. Now which of them will love him more?" Simon answered, "The one, I suppose, to whom he forgave more." And he said to him, "You have judged rightly." Then turning to the woman and said to Simon, "Do you see this woman? I entered your house, you gave me no water for my feet, but she has wet my feet with her tears and wiped them with her hair. You gave me no kiss, but from the time I came in she has not ceased to kiss my feet. You did not anoint my head with oil, but she has anointed my feet with ointment. Therefore I tell you, her sins, which are many, are forgiven, for she loved much; but he who is forgiven little, loves little." And he said to her, "Your sins are forgiven." Then those who were at table with him began to say among themselves, "Who is this, who even forgives sins?" And he said to the woman, "Your faith has saved you; go in peace." (Luke 7:36–50)

If you've ever seen St. Peter's Basilica in Vatican City, you know that it is an immense and imposing structure. Before you even enter the building, the wide-columned arms of St. Peter's Square draw you into the shadow of the facade. Once you get inside, you'll notice that the details and lines of the marble floors and walls all point forward to the towering altar with the famous Holy Spirit window in the background.

I had been to St. Peter's many times, but this time was different. In the center of the church, right in front of the main altar, the body of Pope John Paul II was lying in state. I really can't explain what an honor it was to be able to be at St. Peter's on the first day of viewing. John Paul II had been pope for most of my life, and I was in awe that I was able to be present to pray one last time with the Holy Father.

Given that there were millions of people who also wanted to pay their respects, the Swiss Guards were moving the crowd through rather quickly. I was frustrated. I wanted some time just to be quiet, to be "alone" with the Holy Father, but everyone was being pushed through.

As I got close to the Holy Father, I spied a few kneelers placed off to the right and left side of the Holy Father's body. I was pretty sure they were for VIPs and I was clearly not one, but I asked one of the Swiss Guards if I could kneel and pray for a few minutes. The guard looked incredulous, surprised that I would even ask. "Of course not," was the reply I received. The VIP section was reserved for cardinals, dignitaries, and presidents.

Through a total act of God, just a few minutes after being rejected, I was invited to concelebrate a special Cardinal's Mass behind the main altar, right under the Chair of Peter and that famous Holy Spirit window. I was simply in the right place at the right time to be invited, and it was an honor to concelebrate this Mass for the repose of the soul of John Paul II.

Now this is where the story goes off the rails a bit. As I walked out of the sacristy with the cardinals, I noticed that the VIP section next to the Holy Father's body was empty. It didn't look like there were any cardinals, dignitaries, or presidents around. More importantly, it didn't look like there were any Swiss Guards around!

I realized this was my chance. On one level, I knew I did not belong there, but I just wanted to pray. I just wanted to thank the Holy Father for all he did for the Church, for all he did for me. I had on many occasions received John Paul's priestly blessing and wanted to offer him mine. And besides, I was sure the Holy Father would not have minded.

I kept telling myself, "I just want to pray. They won't stop me from praying!"

Wow, was I wrong! Just as I got to the kneelers and reverently, prayerfully knelt, out of nowhere a Swiss Guard appeared. I felt a tug on the hood of my Franciscan habit, and before I could protest or explain that I was just praying, I was being pulled out of the VIP section. I didn't belong.

The sinful woman in Luke's Gospel account had no business being at that Pharisee's gathering. But this didn't matter to her.

She came to the party because something in the depths of her heart told her that Jesus would never send her away. If she could get to him, if she could just be in the same room, she just knew she would be okay. She simply wanted to be close to him. Perhaps she had heard Jesus preach before, or maybe she had only heard about him from others. Either way, she knew he was different. She knew he approached people like her with love. She trusted him to love and forgive her rather than condemn her.

What's Your Legacy?

That woman in the story will always be remembered as the sinful woman.

How will you be remembered in ten, fifty, or one hundred years? What do you want your legacy to be? I love some of the titles we give to our heroes. We call Saint Joseph "Terror of Demons" and Saint John "The Beloved Disciple." Saint Francis has been remembered as the "Mirror of Christ." Sometimes these nicknames are a little less flattering. Even though the apostle Thomas is a saint and a martyr, he is widely known today as "Doubting Thomas." How about that, you are forever remembered and known for a moment of weakness?

And of course, there are always "the companions." There were twenty-six Christians martyred in Nagasaki on February 5, 1597, but today we refer to the entire group as "Saint Paul Miki and Companions." Are you serious? "A companion?" Imagine being literally killed for your faith and only getting to be a "companion." Lord, have mercy, I am so petty.

At any rate, the woman in the Gospel passage has a legacy as well. Here we are more than two thousand years later, and she is simply remembered as "The Sinful Woman." We don't know much more about her or how her life turned out. We don't even know her name, but we know she shows up uninvited to the party with no business being there. She has an encounter with Jesus which is so intimate and vulnerable I feel as if I should look away, like I shouldn't be there. What is taking place is too personal, too sacred.

She barges into a room where she was not invited or welcome. Her shame leads her to weep at Jesus' feet. Everyone is watching, and I can imagine everyone has that awkward feeling of should we say or do something? The woman falls to the ground and begins kissing Jesus' feet. She rubs ointment on his feet and then takes down her hair and uses it to dry them. A woman would never let down her hair in the presence of a group of men. And drying his feet with it? Scandalous! It's equivalent to a woman taking off her shirt to dry Jesus' feet. She worries not, and at that moment she has no concern about anyone else in the room except him.

The guests start muttering to themselves. They say to each other that if Jesus knew what kind of a woman this was, he wouldn't be letting this happen. But Jesus knows exactly who this woman is. She is a daughter of God. She has sinned greatly, and this has moved her to go to a place she doesn't belong. Her sin moves her to great sorrow, to tears. She weeps for the sins she has committed.

Have you wept for your sins? My guess is that at one time or another, you did something that hurt someone you loved, and this moved you to tears, moved you to apologize. Have you ever had that kind of experience with God? Have you ever turned from God who has always loved you perfectly and been moved to tears when you realized or thought better of it? If you haven't had this happen, I pray you do. And if you are saying you've never really done anything "that bad," you may not quite get it. We have all sinned and fallen short. Apart from God's mercy and the saving work of Jesus, we would all be eternally lost.

I recall a gentleman who had such an encounter. I was leading a group of pilgrims to Guadalupe and was truly blessed by them. There was one man who was so joyful and gregarious. He always sat near the front of the bus and would chat enthusiastically with me, the bus driver, and the other pilgrims.

On the second day we were blessed to be able to visit the shrine of Our Lady of Guadalupe. It is so moving to be with pilgrims from all over Mexico and see their devotion and love of Our Lady. Many of them crawl on their knees the last several blocks to the shrine. You can see in their faces the pain and discomfort, but they keep "walking" on their knees to visit Our Lady. It's also beautiful to see the people finally approach the miraculous tilma. Many of them are weeping as they approach, praying, "Santa Maria, Santa Maria, Santa Maria ..." I have been to most of the major Marian pilgrimage sites, and there is something special about Guadalupe. Our Lady is so humble, so gentle and beautiful. The other major Marian sites are amazing also, but most are in Europe, and Guadalupe is geographically close to us in the USA, our neighbor. The whole experience is so powerful and moving.

As we loaded back on the bus, everyone was in good spirits, but I couldn't see our extroverted friend. I eventually found him near the back of the bus. He was bent over, resting his head on the seat in front of him. At first, I thought he was napping, and then it occurred to me that he was softly weeping. I sat down next to him and asked what was going on. He told me, "Father Dave, my whole life I've been prejudiced against Mexicans. I've judged them and disliked them. I've even treated them unfairly through my business. But today I saw them approach Our Lady with so much zeal, devotion, and love, it just hit me. It was like my sin was right in my face, racism, hatred, judging, it was all right in front of me. I'm so ashamed."

In that shrine, this man had encountered his own brokenness and sin, and it touched him deeply. This encounter with his brokenness would change his life. "I have to change. I can't do this anymore," he shared with me. He couldn't go back to the way he had been. In this moment of encounter with his own brokenness, this man experienced conversion and was drawn closer to Jesus.

He saw where he had failed, where he had a need for Jesus. And Jesus used that moment to affect real change in his life. Jesus met him in his sin, just as he met the woman in the Gospel. He wants to do the same for us.

The sinful woman knew her need. She knew her sin and brokenness and that Jesus could free her. Simon and the others at the party had no sense of this need for God. They didn't see their own sins and shortcomings, and they failed to recognize their need for mercy.

Unfortunately, it's often the same for many of us. All too often we are unaware of our need for God until we want something from him. That woman knew that she was trapped in her life of sin. She knew her need for a Savior. Her encounter with the mercy of God changed her.

It is for this reason that I have a problem with her title "The Sinful Woman." Because after her encounter with Jesus, after her moment of conversion, she is a completely different woman. It seems she shouldn't be called "The Sinful Woman" anymore. Maybe "the party-crashing, Jesus-washing, feet-kissing, ointment-anointing, hair-down-in-public, converted, forgiven woman." I know it doesn't flow as nicely, but it's way more accurate.

Sin-Obsessed

Someone once said to me, "Catholics are obsessed with sin." My response was that we take our lead from Jesus, and if we are obsessed with sin, it's only because Jesus seemed to address the issue often.

At the very beginning of the Gospel of Mark, Jesus announces his mission, saying, "The time is fulfilled, and the kingdom of God is at hand; repent, and believe in the gospel" (Mk 1:15). Remember, the word that Jesus uses here for "repent" is "metanoia," which means to turn or to change. I think it's important to reflect on the reality that the first thing Jesus says to us is to turn away from sin. Later in Mark's Gospel, when Jesus sends out the disciples for the very first time, he tells them to preach repentance (see Mk 6:12). At the very end of both Luke's and John's Gospels, Jesus speaks of repentance and forgiveness of sin. There can be no doubt that Jesus desired men and women to be more aware of their sin so that they could be free from it and know his mercy.

We need to more seriously address our attitude toward sin. It's not enough for us to say to ourselves that we aren't that bad or that others are worse sinners than we are. We need to root out all sin. But we also need to be clear: Sin doesn't keep Jesus away from us. In the Gospels Jesus spends much of his time with sinners. We are reminded that it is for the sinner that Jesus came, not the righteous. Jesus engages sinners, he loves them, eats with them, goes to their homes, and calls them out of their sin to conversion. He never lets them stay in their sin but rather is always telling them to go and sin no more. Jesus was absolutely, 100 percent accepting, loving, and tolerant of every sinful person he met, but he was never accepting, loving, or tolerant of sin, because he knew it was the cause of death.

To that end, I think we need to take sin seriously because Jesus took it seriously. Obviously, as a priest I have an interesting perspective toward sin. Tragically, too many times I've seen the fruits of sin, the effects of sin.

Sin:

- destroys the human person,
- breaks up marriages,
- tears families apart,
- causes some men to prey on women and see them as objects for their pleasure,
- allows people to see those with a different skin color as less than, insignificant, or worthless,
- moves some priests to commit horrible, despicable abuses,

- causes some women to lose concern for their un-born children,
- moves physical intimacy from something holy, beautiful, and life-giving to total self-gratification and use of another person,
- traps people in addictions,
- exploits the beauty of the human body through pornography,
- leads some people to believe that wealth, recognition, power, and worldly goods are the most important things in life,
- leads us to dismiss entire groups of people as less worthy or important,
- leads us to slander and judgment of those we don't desire to understand,
- causes us to speak ill of one another,
- encourages lies and deceit, and
- allows people to become suspicious, cynical, bitter, and closed off to God's grace.

I could go on and on about how sin destroys our relationships with God, ourselves, and others, but I think you get the point. Sin traps us and makes us into something below our dignity as sons and daughters of God. We need to take sin seriously because sin kills the soul. The result of sin that is not repented of is eternal separation from God. Even as I write this it sounds harsh, but it is the reality, and to not address this would be to not speak the whole truth. Jesus spoke of it and so must we.

One thing that we need to be fully aware of is that our ability to recognize our sin is an act of God's mercy. We pray to know our sin so that we can repent and be forgiven and, ultimately, so that we don't have to live and die in the state of sin.

God really does want us to be free from our sin. We can be

different; we can be changed. Conversion is possible for everyone. God brings metanoia; he allows us to turn and change. There may be times when you feel like you are never going to change, like you'll always be impatient, angry, or impure; but don't give up, don't stop begging for God's help. He won't give up on you, so don't give up on him. This is all part of the spiritual life. If we are striving for the things of God, we ought not to be discouraged.

A truth of the spiritual life is that the closer we get to the light, the more we can see. Sometimes what we see is scary and unflattering, and sometimes we just get tired and feel like giving up. But we can't. Conversion is a lifelong process. It's a journey. I love what Pope Francis says: "He [God] never tires of forgiving, but at times we get tired of asking for forgiveness."* Let us pray for the grace to never stop seeking conversion.

His Love for Us

It was my first trip to the Holy Land, and I was excited because the next day I was going to walk the stations of the cross or the *Via Dolorosa*. I could hardly believe that I was going to be able to walk where Jesus walked on his way to crucifixion. I spent the morning in the chapel praying, trying to prepare my heart. I found myself meditating on what it would be like to walk that path, and I had an image of Jesus carrying his cross while I walked alongside him. I could see how badly his body had been beaten. His flesh was torn and bruised. Oddly, the thing that struck me most was where the wood of the cross met his shoulder. The cross was rough, and splinters were digging into Jesus' neck and back. With each step the wood of the cross would rub up and down his neck and shoulders, leaving painful splinters.

As Jesus continued his walk to Golgotha, I sheepishly approached him. I got as close to him as I could and began telling

---

* Pope Francis, Angelus address, March 27, 2013.

him about all the sins I had committed throughout my life. I didn't hold anything back. I would mention a few things and step back awaiting his response. Was he angry? Scandalized? Shocked? Jesus didn't seem horrified about my revelations, almost as if he already knew.

As he kept walking, I began to grow irritated. I asked him, "Why do you keep walking? Why do you keep doing this?" He didn't respond, but just kept walking. Frustrated, I turned around, and that's when I noticed that there was a long line of people I hadn't seen before. As far as I could see there was a line of people waiting to do what I had just done, to confess to Jesus all the sins they had committed. I stepped out of the way.

Fairly quickly I was overwhelmed by the number of people and all their sins, so I turned and yelled one more time, "Jesus, why do you keep walking?" This time he stopped and looked into my eyes and said, "Because I love you." Then he began walking again.

It was a moment of profound grace for me. At that moment I understood, perhaps more clearly than ever before, the nature of my sin and the depths of God's love. Jesus bore my sins and took them to the cross with him. In his death and resurrection, he broke the power of sin and death so that I might live. My prayer is that we all come to know the depths of this reality, that we come to know the nature of our sin so as to know him who surpasses all understanding.

Questions

Continually becoming more aware of our sin is a grace and ought to move us closer to God's heart. What has been your experience of personally encountering the mercy of God?

How would you explain the impact that sin has on the human person?

Metanoia Moment

Come, Lord Jesus. Grant me the grace to recognize my sin, not to judge or condemn myself, but so that I might know your love and mercy.

There is no sin that you have committed that a saint before you hasn't also committed. Saint John says, "God is light and in him is no darkness" (1 Jn 1:5). Take a few minutes and pray that as you work to address sin in your life, you would be overshadowed by God's healing, illuminating light. Ask for the grace to avoid discouragement and despair during this turning away from sin.

CHAPTER 5
JESUS PRAYS

Jesus prayed. He prayed a lot.

It's actually one of the things the Gospels mention most. They specifically indicate Jesus praying over twenty-five times.

Of course, we know that Jesus prayed. I mean, it's obvious that he would pray. But I think it's important to ask how he prayed and why he prayed. There's this perception that Jesus just prayed because, well, that's what he does, he prays.

It reminds me of a note that my niece once wrote to Santa. She made a big card and wrote inside, "Dear Santa, keep on doing what you're doing." We often think that Jesus prayed, well, because that's just what Jesus did.

And it's true, everything that Jesus did, he did in a spirit of prayer. Jesus prayed silently, and he prayed exuberantly. He prayed alone, and he prayed in desolate places. He prayed in the synagogue, and he prayed in the Temple. He prayed before and after he healed. He prayed before and after he spoke. He prayed before he took and broke bread. The key moments in Jesus' life were always related to prayer. He prayed before and as he died.

But *why* did Jesus pray? Why would God need to pray?

Why Did He Pray?

Jesus prayed because he was a good Jew. A devout Jewish man was expected to pray three times daily on a regular day, four times daily on the Sabbath and most Jewish holidays, and five times on Yom Kippur. Jesus prayed as frequently as his fellow Jews would pray. He followed the Jewish observances. He went to the Temple and to the synagogue. He prayed as he should.

Jesus prayed as an example for us. Throughout the Scriptures, Jesus demonstrates different ways of prayer as an example for the people around him. We see this clearly right before he raises his friend Lazarus from the dead. In the story Jesus can be heard saying, "Father, I thank you that you have heard me. I knew that you always hear me, but I have said this on account of the people standing by, that they may believe that you sent me" (Jn 11:41–42). Jesus knows that the crowd is watching and listening, so he prays out loud. His prayer reminds the crowds (and us) that prayer is important.

But most importantly, Jesus prayed because he wanted to be in relationship with his Father. Jesus was completely dependent on his heavenly Father and said that without the Father, he could do nothing. In John's Gospel he made it clear that he can only do what he sees the Father doing (see Jn 5:19; 5:30; 8:28). I think this is a powerful image. Jesus as Son follows the lead of his Father, and it was prayer that allowed him to know this. The Son imitates the Father, and Jesus' life of prayer was a life of paying attention. He looked for signs and directions from the Father and followed where the Father led.

If Jesus needed to pray and have this communion with the Father, how much more do we need to pray?

Why do we pray? Do you pray? I mean really pray, time set aside where you do your best to focus your undivided attention on the Lord? This is different from an occasional "Lord, help me," or, "Find my keys." Not that those are bad prayers (they are not), but there needs to be something more.

Maybe a better question is, Why don't we pray? What keeps us from spending some time with the Lord? Are we too busy? Do we not know how to pray? Do we believe it matters? These are all good questions that need to be settled. But what is important is that we are honest about our relationship with God and are willing to explore that perhaps there is more to prayer than what we are experiencing.

For most people prayer is primarily asking for things. Be honest, how much of your prayer, maybe a percentage, is asking God for stuff? Is it 30, 40, 50 percent or more? To be clear, God wants us to do this, and we will deal with it more later, but it's not the only reason we pray. While it's important to ask for things from God, we can sometimes make that the only thing we do in prayer. We make requests, beg, coerce, and try to use prayer as a way to bargain with God. Our prayer can sometimes be motivated by fear or superstition. "Lord, I am going to fast today because I really need …" We've all been there.

Recently, I went on a pilgrimage to Fátima in Portugal. While I was there, I learned about a prayer tradition that the locals have to Saint Anthony. Apparently, when a single girl decides it is time to get married, she asks Saint Anthony to help her. So far, so good. However, if Saint Anthony is taking too long to find that husband, the woman puts a statue of Saint Anthony upside down in a bucket of water and leaves him there until he finds her a husband. That sounds kind of crazy, until it works.

Our prayer isn't, or shouldn't be, about making God do what we want. The ultimate point of prayer isn't to cure illnesses, get raises, or find eligible Portuguese bachelors. We pray because we need intimacy with God.

I don't think there has ever been a time in my life when prayer was not important to me. Now, there have been lots of times in my life when I have not been faithful to prayer, when I have just gone through the motions and have needed to refocus on the necessity of prayer. But prayer has been a long, constant friend of mine. Maybe I didn't always feel like praying, but something in me always realized that prayer was important. There is something necessary about just sitting in prayer and being available to God. Maybe not saying a lot of words but just being quiet.

The importance of prayer became clearer to me when I was in seminary. I was spending my summer at a parish in Fort Worth. I remember walking into the parish office on a Monday morning and there was a gentleman who was extremely angry. He was livid because he had stopped by the parish office on Saturday afternoon at around 2:00 p.m., and there was no one in the office. (The offices are closed on Saturday.) He was irate that there was not a priest at the office whenever he needed one. I found myself wondering, "What is reasonable to expect from our priests? Is it reasonable to expect a priest to be at the parish office twenty-four hours a day? Is it reasonable to expect that a priest always has the right answer? Is it reasonable to expect a priest never to be grouchy, angry, shy? Is it reasonable to expect priests to be perfect?"

I spent a long time over a couple of days thinking about this question. What can the people of God expect of priests? There are of course probably lots of things, but what came to me at that time was that it was reasonable to expect priests to pray. The priest should be a man of deep prayer. You should expect that we pray and seek a deeper relationship with our Father. You should expect that our lives give witness to Jesus by our prayer. Priests might not always be perfect, but we should always be striving for this, and we should be seeking the grace of prayer to aid us.

As a priest it's also my responsibility to pray for the community that the Lord has given me to shepherd. Much of my time in prayer is taking with me the cares, worries, and sufferings of my people. I stand in the gap for the people and seek the Lord's blessing for them. This is something that we can all do for one another. What a gift to give to someone to take them to prayer with you. It's a beautiful expression of your care and concern for another.

Teach Us How to Pray

Okay, so prayer is important. But *how* do we pray? When the disciples see Jesus pray, this is their question to him. They ask him, "Lord, teach us to pray" (Lk 11:1). God desires to teach us how to pray. Ultimately, we learn how to pray the same way we would learn how to ride a bike, play an instrument, practice a sport, begin a hobby, or drive a car. We learn with practice. There is a connection between our commitment to praying and how "well" we pray.

I don't want this book to be a how-to prayer guide. There are already plenty of books on that, trying to tell you the perfect way to pray. There are many different theories, styles, and methods of prayer. The Benedictines will tell you that prayer has 138 elements, while the Jesuits and the Dominicans will debate whether it's forty-five or fifty-six elements. I prefer the Franciscan answer — we like to keep it simple.

Prayer is simply a conversation with God, and we need to go into that conversation open and emptied.

One evening a younger friar was sitting outside the door of the cell where Saint Francis was praying. He had his ear to the door, wondering what the saint said when he prayed. The young friar could hear Francis repeating the same thing over and over: "My God and my all." This is so simple and insightful. Prayer doesn't have to be complicated and lots of words, just truthful and personal.

When he talks about prayer, Saint Josemaría Escrivá says, "Put yourselves in the presence of your Father and tell him this much at least: 'Lord, I don't know how to pray. I can't think of anything to tell you.' You can be sure that at that very moment you have already begun to pray."*

Prayer doesn't have to be deep or complicated; what's vitally important is that you be real and honest with God. If you don't have much to say, just tell him! Your conversation with God can be as easy as a conversation with your best friend. Sometimes you might have a lot to say, sometimes he might have a lot to say, and sometimes neither of you will say much at all. Have you ever noticed how some elderly married couples will just sit with each other for hours on a park bench or in the living room without saying a word? For them, a lot of chatter doesn't necessarily equal intimacy. They are happy just being in each other's presence. Sometimes it's the same with prayer. The words are not nearly as important as the time spent together. Prayer is time for you and God to be in each other's presence and have a conversation — big or small!

Another important element to remember in prayer is about letting go. Oftentimes we go to God wanting to be filled or to receive, but we should also use that time to let go. Scripture says, "Cast all your anxieties on him" (1 Pt 5:7). This is a really important part of prayer. Ask God to help you identify your concerns, your worries, hopes, and dreams, and then offer them to the Lord. Trust him and give all you have and all you are.

You don't have to go into prayer with anything on your agenda other than being present to God. Prayer is a process of being emptied so that we may be filled. As we make ourselves small and emptied before God, he will build us up. In prayer we can rid ourselves of the attachments, fears, worries, and sins that keep us from God, and make space to be filled with the Holy Spirit. Being filled with the Spirit of God is much more attractive than being full of fear.

---

* Saint Josemaría Escrivá, *Friends of God* (Strongsville, OH: Scepter, 2017), 145.

Where Is He?

We grow in our relationship with the Lord when we discover that he is always already present to us. When we go to pray, it is good to recall that God is already there. Sure, we may have to work through distractions, but God is with us. By the grace of our baptism, God actually dwells in us. Paul reminds us that Christ has made his dwelling in us (see Rom 8:10). Just knowing this should have a profound impact on our prayer. Because God dwells in us already, prayer is not this epic quest to find God "out there."

I think this is one of the things many people discovered when they were quarantined because of COVID-19. People are accustomed to "going" to church to pray. We go to bible studies, we go to prayer meetings, and we go to adoration, but churches being closed and quarantine changed the way many people prayed. They were invited to discover God in the very place they were.

Prayer is a rediscovery of Christ who already makes his dwelling both with and within us. This is why we pray "in the name of Jesus," because Christ dwells in us and he gives us access to the Father. Here's what the *Catechism of the Catholic Church* has to say about that: "There is no other way of Christian prayer than Christ. Whether our prayer is communal or personal, vocal or interior, it has access to the Father only if we pray 'in the name' of Jesus. The sacred humanity of Jesus is therefore the way by which the Holy Spirit teaches us to pray to God our Father" (2664).

This is good news for us, because it means that Jesus helps us to pray. Just like the disciples, we can ask Jesus to "teach us how to pray," and he will. His dwelling within us allows us to seek intimacy with the Father and the Holy Spirit.

This is what prayer is. It's seeking intimacy with God. It's desiring to know him and experience being known by him. In the Letter to the Hebrews, we read that no one is concealed from God, but everyone is naked and exposed to his eyes (see Heb 4:13). This might sound a little intense, and it is, but it's a good type of intense.

When Adam and Eve fell, one of the first things they did was to cover themselves and then hide from God (see Gn 3:7). I don't want to do that. I don't want to approach God hiding behind my shame, fear, and brokenness; I just want to go before him as I am.

When we can be consistent in our prayer, we begin to encounter him more and to recognize his presence more. Then a wonderful thing begins to happen: This spills out of our prayer. We discover God in places where in the past we missed him. It could be in the Scriptures, the Mass, a family member, or crazy as it sounds, the cross. God is present to us, and I am totally convinced he wants to make this known to us.

A Rule of Life

Prayer will make our daily life better, but where do we put prayer in our daily lives? I remember talking once with a young college student about prayer time. He proudly told me, "Saint Paul says to pray always (see 1 Thes 5:16–18), so I just do that. I'm always praying so don't really set any times aside." Although I affirmed him in his desire to pray always, I also pointed out that it's important to put some time aside.

I'm not really concerned about the specifics of when you pray. Things like time, duration, and place, that's all between you and God. You know yourself — just work out something that works for you. Also, don't be afraid to mix things up a bit. If you're having difficulties, try a different time or place.

When figuring out what your prayer might look like, take in all of the various options: Morning and evening offerings, daily Mass, Liturgy of the Hours, Rosaries, Divine Mercy Chaplets, stations of the cross, a work of mercy, or an hour of adoration are all beautiful options. However, it is a rare person who is called to do all of them. Practice a few devotions and do them well.

Perhaps just start out with one or two things — maybe it's spending a few minutes with the daily Mass readings and then some quiet time. It's easier to be faithful in these small things first.

With that being said, I do find it helpful to have a type of "bare minimum" of prayer that you commit to doing each and every day. What does this mean? Well, it means that sometimes life gets busy and things begin to move in on our allotted time for prayer. I think it's wise to have something that you make absolutely, 100 percent sure you do each and every day, no matter what. It may be shorter and simpler than a typical prayer time, but at least do something, even during the craziness that is so often life.

There are also benefits to establishing some kind of ritual. I personally like my prayer time to follow a basic pattern. First, I recognize that God is present. It seems obvious, but it's good for me to just remind myself, "God, you are here."

I then make an examination of conscience. Just asking the Lord to show you where you have sinned is a wonderful practice. Get this out of the way at the beginning and then continue time with the Lord.

For the thanksgiving part, I call to mind all the gifts and good things God has given me. Some days this list is long, some days it's short. You don't have to come up with a list of every possible thing you have to be grateful for, but it's good to take the time to see where God is blessing you in your life. Another step that is nice every now and then is to make a point of letting someone know you are grateful for them. If someone comes to your mind, drop them a text or a note and let them know they are special to you.

Next, I read Scripture. You don't have to overthink what you read. Some people like to read a new psalm every day or focus on the daily Scripture readings for Mass. Others like to work through a particular Gospel or book of the Bible. Whatever you choose, just be sure to take your time on the passages you read. You don't have to speed through. If a phrase or word is sticking out to you, just focus on that. Lots of people like to use different methods of *lectio divina* — a type of praying with Scripture — while reading the Bible. If that sounds like something you'd like to try, just look it up. There are plenty of *lectio divina* methods to choose from.

It's nice to have a journal with you as you pray. Sometimes something or someone comes to your mind, and it's nice to jot that down. God speaks to me a lot through what I write in my journal.

I like to close prayer with a time of petition. This is a good time to pray for all those people you promised to pray for. Some people like to keep a list of intentions and pray specific prayers to go with them. Some of us less organized folks prefer to stick to something like, "Lord bless (name them) and please help all the people I promised to pray for. Amen." Whatever works for you that allows you to offer petitions to the Lord and connects you with the people you want to pray for is great.

Finally, there are seasons of prayer throughout our lives. Honestly, the quarantine time was possibly the best eight-week period of prayer that I have had in years. Life slowed down just a bit, I didn't travel anywhere, and it was a really blessed time. It is typical that our prayer does not always look the same. The prayer of a five-year-old looks very different from the prayer of a twenty-five-year-old or fifty-year-old. The prayer of a young mom won't be the same as the prayer of a grandmother or college student. My brother has four kids, a wife, and a full-time job, and his prayer life is just a bit different than what mine looks like as a Franciscan friar. In each season of life, it is important for you to understand what kind of prayer life God might be calling you to and embrace the opportunity for deeper intimacy with God within your own state of life. It's okay if your prayer looks different from season to season; the important thing is that you're praying.

Don't overthink it. Prayer isn't something that you have to do perfectly, it's relationship with God. We don't pray to get a gold star on our Catholic report card. We pray because Jesus prayed and told us to pray as well. Jesus sought intimacy with the Father, and so should we. There is a great peace and comfort that comes from a deeper union with the God of Love. We pray because we want this union. We pray because we desire a deeper conversion in our hearts. We pray because Jesus prayed.

Questions

Why do you (or don't you) pray?

Our prayer life might look different in different seasons. How does your prayer life look right now?

How has prayer helped you get to know God better? Has prayer changed how you see God? How do you talk to God?

Metanoia Moment

Come, Holy Spirit.

Take a moment to sit in silence before God the Father. Know that he is looking upon you with love. Reflect on that knowledge that the Father is present to you and is looking at you with love for as long as you want. Imagine the Father repeating the words he spoke of Jesus to you: "You are my beloved son/daughter; with you I am well pleased" (see Lk 3:22).

CHAPTER 6

I AM THE BREAD
OF LIFE

We've all been hungry before. But, of course, there is hunger, and then there is real hunger. When we are *really* hungry, the thought of food is never far from us. When we're truly hungry, all our thoughts go to food — when are we going to eat next, what are we going to eat, where are we going to eat. Sometimes we might just eat a candy bar or other small snack to satisfy our hunger, knowing that it is a temporary fix. Eventually, we know that we are going to need to eat a real meal, something substantial that will satisfy.

If we are hungry for too long, it impacts how we act. We become impatient, rude, or grouchy. And for those who are really hungry, starving even, they become frantic, desperate, and frightened. All the starving person can think about is satisfying their hunger. Over time, that hunger will become a physical pain. Human beings will do crazy and horrifying things to get rid of that pain.

The human heart is no different when it comes to non-physical hunger. Our heart has a tremendous appetite. We have been created with a hunger, a longing, and a sense of being incomplete. We generally recognize bodily hunger, and we know what to do to satisfy that hunger. But the hunger of the heart, the soul's hunger for God — this is different, and many people are unaware of it. Well, maybe more accurately, they know there is a hunger, but they may not be able to identify it or put it into words. It's part of what it means to be human.

Just like we will do crazy things to satisfy our stomach when we experience bodily hunger, we will do some crazy things to try to satisfy our hungry heart. We attempt to fill it with possessions, power, recognition, popularity, being liked ... the list is endless. But these things always leave us wanting and needing more. When this ache isn't satiated, we become frantic. The hunger gets worse. The more we try to satisfy it and fail, the more we wonder if anything will help. We begin to think that maybe we'll always feel this way: empty, frustrated, alone. This is a terribly destructive cycle in which to be trapped.

Yes, every person on earth experiences hunger in their bodies and in their hearts. Only Jesus can satisfy both physical and spiritual hunger.

Everyone Is Following Jesus

Seriously, in John's Gospel everyone is following Jesus. By chapter 6, Jesus is the hottest rabbi in all of Galilee. *"Have you seen him? Have you heard him?"* Everyone is talking about Jesus because of the amazing, miraculous things he is doing. He's performing signs and wonders and preaching with authority. The people are eating it up.

In his Gospel, John tells us about one day when Jesus has been preaching, healing, and teaching. Of course, there are crowds of people around him. Eventually, Jesus wants to get away from the crowds and needs some alone time. So he gets in a boat and goes across the Sea of Galilee.

What happens next is kind of funny to imagine. Once Jesus' boat is underway, the entire crowd of people assembles on the shore and starts to follow the boat all the way around the Sea of Galilee. These people are not going to let Jesus go easy. Jesus and his disciples lose the boat and climb a mountain, but the crowd still follows him.

Looking at the crowd, Jesus figures they must be hungry. They've spent the day walking around the sea and up a mountain without anything to eat. So, he gathers the people, takes five barley loaves and two fish, blesses the food, and feeds the people. John emphasizes the fact that the crowd eats their fill, and there is even bread left over. The people have their physical hunger satisfied, but that's not the only hunger Jesus had come to satisfy.

After feeding the people, Jesus once again tries to get away from the crowd by getting back in a boat and sailing to Capernaum. The crowds follow yet again and surround him. Jesus understands what they are looking for and proclaims, "You seek me, not because you saw signs, but because you ate your fill of the loaves. Do not labor for the food which perishes, but for the food which endures to eternal life" (Jn 6:26–27).

Take a second and let those words of Jesus penetrate your heart. Why do we follow him? Why do we pray, go to Mass, and do good things? Is there a part of us that does these things just because we want good things in return? Are we just doing it because we want to be filled in one way or another? Are we expecting him to give us health, wealth, or worldly power and recognition? Do we follow him for no other reason than he has captured our heart? No doubt we ought to seek Jesus for what he wants to give us, but let's not lose sight of how he longs to fill our soul.

The World Won't Fill Us

A friend of mine once shared that he always wanted to be a doctor. The first step in this long process was that he got into the prestigious college he craved and got outstanding grades. But this never satisfied him; he was surprised of the emptiness but kept working toward his goal. He figured that once he became a resident, with an MD behind his name, he would be able to rest. That didn't work either. Maybe a coveted fellowship? Still empty. Finally, he was in the middle of a lucrative practice having all that he had ever hoped for, and he had never felt so empty. The longing and emptiness moved to frustration and fear. *Perhaps there isn't anything that is going to satisfy.* His life began to spiral out of control leading to drugs and alcohol. He watched his life, all he had worked for, crumble before him.

Or think about the Super Bowl champion who woke up the morning after the game with a deep feeling of emptiness. He had just attained the pinnacle of his career, and what did he feel? Emptiness that left him stating, "This is it? That's all? Now what?"

It can be a frightening experience to discover that the things of the world cannot totally satisfy us. But it is also one of the most liberating. There is a tremendous freedom that comes with the recognition that the world will ultimately fail to satisfy us. Once we come to this reality, it's as if we can stop searching and wondering, and we don't have to keep looking. It's similar to the relief that you feel when you find something. You know what it's like to have lost your keys, and you frantically search until you find them. There is a tremendous relief. It's the same here — there is a relief in "finding" or "discovering" that your ultimate happiness cannot be found in the world.

Beatitude Hunger

In Matthew's Gospel, maybe a mile or two from where Jesus confronted the crowds at Capernaum, Jesus gives us the Beatitudes. He says, "Blessed are those who hunger and thirst for righteousness, for they shall be satisfied" (Mt 5:6). We miss the full meaning of this in English. In the Greek the appropriate way to say that you hunger or thirst for something is you "hunger for a part of" or "thirst for a part of." In Greek you wouldn't say that you "hunger for bread" as in all bread, but that you hunger for a "part of bread."

But in this beatitude, Jesus says it differently. He doesn't say, "Blessed are those who hunger and thirst for a share or a part of righteousness." He says, "Blessed are those who hunger and thirst for *all righteousness.*" Jesus doesn't just want us to have a piece, he wants to give us all of it.

If we are honest with ourselves, I think we have to admit that sometimes we only hunger for a piece of holy things. We want to be holy most of the time. We want to be loving toward a percentage of the people we meet. We want to forgive some people. But we can't just have a partial desire for the Lord and for holiness. We must desire it wholeheartedly. We have to want all of it, not just a piece. We must have that beatitude hunger for the Lord.

Do we have that kind of hunger for God? Do we have that kind of hunger for the things of God? Do we hunger for truth, mercy, purity, compassion, and other virtues?

This hunger in our soul is never-ending. It can be appeased, but it won't go away completely this side of heaven. This kind of hunger can't be satisfied by small spiritual snacks like a few minutes of prayer or listening to some praise and worship music. This kind of hunger can only be satisfied by a total surrender to God. However, the really beautiful thing about God is that he always accepts what we can offer him and makes something beautiful from it. I have totally surrendered my life to God hundreds, thousands of times, and my prayer is that each time I do give my life to him, it is a more complete surrender. Give to the Lord what you are able, and the Lord will delight in your gift.

God will satisfy the hunger of our hearts, but we will not be filled to the point of not wanting more. I am always so excited to go to Mexican restaurants that offer chips and salsa. I go through those chips like a wood chipper, crumbs hurling to the tables next to me. I could eat, and have eaten multiple bowls of chips. When my enchiladas eventually come, I am aware that it's possible I overdid it just a bit. By the time I'm done, I'm so stuffed that I never want to see another bowl of chips and salsa again … until the next time I go to the restaurant.

But God's satisfaction is more perfect than anything this world can offer. God satisfies us, and yet we long for more. We never get too full. When we taste and encounter the Lord, we are not satiated. We are overcome by goodness and desire more. Saint Augustine sums it up perfectly: "You called, you shouted, and you broke through my deafness. You flashed, you shone, and you dispelled my blindness. You breathed your fragrance on me; I drew in breath and now I pant for you. I have tasted you, now I hunger and thirst for more. You touched me, and I burned for your peace."* When we taste the Lord, we want more of him. There is a hunger and thirst in us that only Christ can satisfy.

Fulfilled in Christ

Jesus comes to quench our thirst. In John's Gospel he says, "If any one thirst, let him come to me and drink. He who believes in me, as the Scripture has said, 'Out of his heart shall flow rivers of living water'" (Jn 7:37–38). Earlier, Jesus says a very similar thing to the woman at the well: "Every one who drinks of this water will thirst again; but whoever drinks of the water that I shall give him will never thirst; the water that I shall give him will become in him a spring of water welling up to eternal life" (Jn 4:13–14).

I recall one time giving a homily on the power of the Word of God and how God's Word can speak to us and give life. The Word of God is alive, and it can penetrate the depths of our heart. It can

---

* Saint Augustine, Office of Readings, August 28.

heal, free, and transform an individual who is open. At the end of Mass, I was approached by an elderly woman. She shared that she was a recent widow, having been married for over fifty years.

She went on to explain that one of the most difficult times for her had been attending Mass:

> My husband and I went to Mass every Sunday for over fifty years. Attending Mass without him was terrible. I felt most alone at Mass, which bothered me. Well, a few years ago I was attending Mass and the Gospel was the Woman at the Well. I listened to the words of Jesus to the woman, him telling her that he can give water so that she would never thirst again. Father Dave, I don't know what came over me, but I said, "Jesus, I want that water!" What happened next changed me, and I have never been the same. I experienced a feeling of water flowing over me like a waterfall. I wasn't merely drinking the water, I was being bathed in it. From that moment on, I have not had the deep emptiness. Sure, I miss my husband, but it changed that day. And the best thing is that I once again loved coming to Mass, and in a strange way I now feel closest to my husband here.

This is what an encounter with Christ does to our hearts: It changes us for the good. Jesus completely drenches us in his love, and we walk away changed forever.

To Whom Shall We Go?

In the midst of not being able to attend liturgy during the COVID shutdown in 2020, I think this was the prayer of many people: "Lord, to whom shall we go?" Not being able to receive the Eucharist for many people was terribly difficult. Many people spoke of the hunger for Jesus in the Eucharist. I believe that this may be one of the greatest graces to come from this whole tragedy: a deeper love and desire for Jesus in the Eucharist. We knew we were hungry, but it wasn't until we were not able to receive Jesus that the full reality hit us.

Jesus knew all along.

In the synagogue in Capernaum he says, "I am the living bread which came down from heaven; if anyone eats of this bread, he will live forever" (Jn 6:51). "I am the bread of life. Your fathers ate the manna in the wilderness, and they died" (Jn 6:48–49). "Truly, truly, I say to you, unless you eat the flesh of the Son of Man and drink his blood, you have no life in you; he who eats my flesh and drinks my blood has eternal life" (Jn 6:53–54).

Jesus had said some off-the-wall things before, but this was over the top. And Jesus is aware of this, he gets it. Jesus knows that this is a hard teaching. He watches as the crowd slowly disperses. Many of Jesus' followers end up leaving him.

"Will you also leave?" he asks his apostles. He knows that many people will go looking somewhere else and will ultimately be left empty. But he lets them go; they must discover this on their own.

Peter answers him, "Lord, to whom shall we go? You have the words of eternal life; and we have believed, and have come to know, that you are the Holy One of God" (Jn 6:68–69). It was clear to Saint Peter that apart from Jesus there was no real life.

This sounds odd, but how wonderfully godly this is. Jesus knows we will hunger, so he takes simple bread, the food of the common man that fills the hunger of our stomachs. Then, from what can only be a God thing, by the power of his Holy Spirit, he transforms the bread for the stomach to life for the soul. By taking and eating, we participate in eternal life and our hearts are fed.

Take a moment and make Peter's prayer your own.

Lord, to whom will I go?

When I am lonely, frustrated, or angry, to whom will I go?

When I am empty, disappointed, and feeling abandoned, where will I turn?

When I am broken, trapped, and discouraged, where will I go?

When I am filled with joy and peace, to whom will I go?

Help me turn to you, Lord. Make my heart like Peter's and help me believe that you are the Holy One of God. Help me to know that you are the only one who can satisfy my hunger.

The more we can pray something like this, the more we understand our need for God and are filled with hope, knowing that he will fulfill our deepest need.

Questions

We have been created hungry. How have you experienced God satisfying this hunger?

What do you look to other than God to satisfy your hunger?

When are you most hungry?

Metanoia Moment

Come, Holy Spirit.

When Jesus asked his disciples if they too would leave, they responded, "Lord, to whom shall we go? You have the words of eternal life; and we have believed, and have come to know, that you are the Holy One of God" (Jn 6:68–69). Ask the Holy Spirit to make these words of the disciples the prayer of your own heart. Take these moments to turn to God with your own loneliness, fears, frustrations, and feelings. Allow yourself to encounter God as an intimate friend to whom you can go.

CHAPTER 7
CALLED AND CHOSEN

I've long joked that I was going to write a book on what they did not teach us in seminary. Believe me, it would be a long book, because most of my experiences since I have been a priest we never discussed when I was in seminary.

I was in a country where Christianity was largely oppressed and wanted to see some of the sites in the city where I was staying. My host, Sister Mary, arranged a guide for me. Robin* was a friend of my host, knew the local city, and was able to speak English. In the afternoon I wanted to see what a local church looked like. Robin thought she knew where one was and took me to the church. While I was praying, she tapped me on the shoulder and asked if I would pray that her daughter would come to faith. I said I would be happy to, but I thought her request was odd, given that she herself was not a Christian.

The next day I was in a meeting and Robin was a part of the gathering. Robin's question had me wondering how converts are

---

* Not her real name.

brought into the Church in a communist country. So I asked Sister Mary how people are brought into the Church without an RCIA program? At that moment Robin jumped up and exclaimed, "I want to be baptized; I want to be a Christian."

Here is where my seminary let me down; not once did we deal with what to do if your tour guide in a communist, anti-Christian country wants to be baptized. Not even once!

Sister Mary looked at Robin then at me and stated, "It's up to you, Father." So, after a few hours of discernment and discussions with Robin and Sister, we decided that Robin would be baptized. It was one of the most beautiful experiences ever. In a small make-shift chapel, with about ten people, Robin was baptized, the tears flowing from her cheeks mixing with the waters of baptism. She was radiant as the water was poured over her head.

We had a small reception after the baptism, and with tears still in her eyes Robin exclaimed, "Father Dave, today is a dream come true." She then went on to share with me the first time she had heard about Jesus. She was a little girl living in a small village and a preacher was moving through the area. "He read out of a book — I now know it was the Bible — 'It was not you who chose me, it was I who chose you.' I heard the man read that and thought to myself, 'I wish I had been chosen, I wish he had chosen me.' Father Dave, today I have finally been chosen, he chose me. It's a dream come true!"

In the deepest part of our hearts, we all just want to be chosen. In Christ everyone is loved, seen, known, and chosen. I have been chosen. You have been chosen. Sadly, many people don't know this or believe it. Our hearts and minds need to be changed and come to an understanding of the reality that God chooses us.

Pick Me!

Everyone wants to be picked. We all want someone to look at us and say, "I want you." We desire to be recognized, to be seen, to be noticed.

This is why some people hate high school homecoming or prom — it is so hard waiting and wondering, "Is anyone going to ask me? Does anyone want me?" Others hated recess for the same reason. I remember recess as a kid when we would play kick-ball. We'd all line up and begin to pick teams, and many would be thinking the same thing: "Am I going to be picked? Who's going to pick me?" There was one boy in my class named Max, and he had a problem with his legs and had to wear heavy braces. He didn't run as fast as the other kids and was always picked last for sports; he didn't like recess very much.

In my junior year I went out for the baseball team. I played baseball a lot growing up, and I had made the team the previous years of high school, so I went into the tryouts confident. The day of cuts came, and all the guys went into the locker room to see who had been cut. On a large poster board were the names of all the guys who had tried out. A line divided the poster. Those whose names were above the line made the team, below the line meant you were cut. I had never been cut before, so my eyes scanned above the line. My name was not there. I had been cut. I wasn't good enough. I was not chosen. I couldn't believe it — I had never been cut from anything. I was frustrated, angry, embarrassed, sad, and a whole bunch of other feelings. I felt kind of lost. I had played baseball every spring since I was a little kid. What now? I felt like a failure.

So many things in our life are about being chosen. Will you be accepted to that college? Will you receive that job, promotion, or raise? Will you meet a special someone? Will she want to marry you? We look to others to decide if we're wanted or not. We look to others to tell us what we're worth.

I once knew a young woman who *really* wanted to be married. Every time we met, she would talk about this desire. Her desire to be seen, to be chosen, was consuming her. She was afraid to move forward in her life and make decisions. She weighed every decision according to this one criterion: "Will this bring me closer to finding someone to marry?" One day we were praying together, and I stated: "You are not a piece of fruit, merely to be picked." At that moment she became emotional. You see, I had the sense that she was waiting around and hoping for someone to pick her off the proverbial tree. She was waiting for someone to see her, to choose her, to give her purpose, meaning, and peace. She was totally paralyzed and was not fully living. This was a profound moment of metanoia for her.

We often do this. We wait around hoping that someone will see us and bestow value on us. We can do this with anyone in our life, be it a boss, a superior, a parent, a spouse, or someone else. When we live like this, we give others the ability to determine our worth. The coach who oversaw our baseball tryouts determined I was not good enough to make the team. Fair enough. But this gets more difficult when we view all of our lives in terms of others choosing us, allowing other people not merely to determine if we are talented enough, but to define us. There is a significant difference between thinking, "I was not good enough to make the team" and thinking, "I am not enough." One speaks to my ability and one to my worth. One may in fact be true: I didn't play well enough! And one is a destructive lie.

It's essential that we not give others the power to define us or to determine our worth. No coach, teacher, superior, or boss determines my worth. Honestly, I don't even determine that for myself! God alone makes this determination. I am created in the image and likeness of God, and it is here that I find my deepest understanding of who I am.

From the very beginning God chooses us. He literally chooses us into existence. God chooses humanity and has from the beginning of time. God didn't have to create humanity; no one forced him. But he freely chose to create, and his creation of us is a choice *for* us. His choice to create us brings us into existence, and his choice to sustain us in creation is another choice for us, another yes to us. At every moment of our lives, God is choosing us. In baptism we are again reminded that we are chosen. The baptized are forever united in Christ and once again chosen.

I think often we see being chosen as a singular event, but it doesn't work like that with God. He is always eternally choosing us. Even in the midst of our brokenness and sin, God still chooses us. You are his beloved, and nothing you do could cause God to stop choosing you.

God would eventually choose humanity in a most radical way through the Incarnation. When Jesus takes flesh, he chooses to become one of us. He chooses to be human. God makes a choice to forever unite himself to our humanity. He did not have to do this, but he chose to. In Jesus the Father forever says yes to humanity. This choosing affirms and restores human nature as well as our beauty and dignity, which had been compromised in the Fall. Because Jesus is the perfect human, he perfectly restores humanity. Humanity is made whole again in Christ. But God does not merely choose "humanity" in a general sense; he also chooses each one of us. He chooses me. He chooses you. It's always personal.

The Gospel Truth

We see this personal choosing in the Gospels. In the Gospel of Mark, we meet a blind man named Bartimaeus, who is sitting by the road as Jesus is passing by. He begins to cry out to Jesus, begging for mercy. Jesus stops and commands the crowd to call Bartimaeus to him. They tell him, "Take heart; rise, he is calling you" (Mk 10:49). Jesus is calling Bartimaeus to himself, ultimately calling him out of his blindness into light.

I love this text. Jesus asks Bartimaeus, "What do you want me to do for you?" (Mk 10:51). I think it would have been obvious what Bartimaeus was hoping for. He was plainly blind — of course he wanted to see! But Jesus asks him to speak his need out loud; he wants him to say it, to verbalize it. There is a vulnerability, a step in faith, an experience of conversion when we have the courage to put into words our need for God. We put it out there, praying, hoping, asking, and all the while not knowing what God will do. But we are honest with the Lord because he asks us what we want.

"Let me receive my sight" (Mk 10:51). Jesus calls Bartimaeus out of darkness and into his light. Bartimaeus is seen, healed, chosen.

Zacchaeus also desperately wants to see Jesus. He is a bit of an outcast in his town, and no one likes him much because he's a tax collector. He lives on the margins of society, is never invited to parties, and has no friends. Zacchaeus is not a popular guy.

But Jesus is amazingly popular, and everywhere he goes is an event. In his desperation to see Jesus, Zacchaeus climbs a tree in the middle of the square to see him. In the midst of the commotion, Jesus sees Zacchaeus and calls out, "Zacchaeus, make haste and come down; for I must stay at your house today" (Lk 19:5). Jesus sees Zacchaeus and calls him by name, choosing to be with him and to go to his home.

I love the crowd's reaction: They start to complain! Jesus is going to stay at a sinner's house. All the crowd can see is Zacchaeus's sin, but Jesus sees Zacchaeus. Jesus sees past his sins to call him as a person, and he calls him out of his sin.

Zacchaeus responds to being chosen. He jumps out of the tree, stands before Jesus, and promises to give half of his possessions to the poor. He repents of any sins and promises to repay those he extorted four times over (see Lk 19:8).

In that moment, in his simple encounter with Jesus, Zacchaeus's life is forever changed. Jesus speaks to his heart. "I want to have dinner at your house. I know your life is a mess, but I can fix that. I want to be with you." Zacchaeus responds to this invitation and is changed. This is the key to conversion. You can't respond to

God's call to metanoia without a willingness to change, and this is so often the stumbling block for us. We don't like change. We don't like to be told we are doing something wrong. We get comfortable and resist having to change what we do. If our lives are going to be conformed to Christ, if we are going to respond to being chosen, we have got to be willing to let him change us. He calls us out of our blindness and our sin, and answering his call means we will be changed.

It's not just blindness and sin that Jesus will call us out of; it's also death.

Jesus is standing before a tomb and cries out in a loud voice, commanding Lazarus to come out (see Jn 11:43). Entirely wrapped and tied up in the burial cloths, Lazarus obliges. By the power of his word, Jesus calls Lazarus out of death and into life. He sees how he is held bound, first by the tomb and then by the burial cloths. Jesus restores him to life and then tells the crowd to untie him from the cloths, so that he may be fully free. It's essential we understand this about Jesus. Jesus not only makes sad people happy and blind people see, he brings the dead to life. He calls each of us into new life, into a new way of being.

When we are chosen, we are chosen *from* something into a life with Christ. Bartimaeus is called out of his blindness. Zacchaeus is called out of his sin. Lazarus is called out of his tomb itself. We may be called from anger to forgiveness or fear to courage, but there is always movement to conversion. What is Jesus calling you from and what is he calling you to?

Called Out and Called For

Christ's choosing us is an eternal choosing. He doesn't just choose us once or choose us at our best moment. He chooses us at every moment. Think about the worst moment in your life, the moment where you feel you were at your absolute worst. Even right in that moment, God was choosing you.

I love this image of Jesus continually choosing us. This is beautiful because it is the deepest desire of every human heart to be chosen. We want to be chosen as a kid in sports, theater, or band. We want to be chosen for that great college, job, promotion, or seat on the board. We are starving for someone to see us and know us. We want others to recognize and affirm our worth, goodness, and beauty. We want to be seen. We want to be chosen. We want to be called. But no human being can perfectly see us the way we really want to be seen. Our parents, spouses, and close friends can and often do meet us in the mess of our life, and this is a grace given to us from the Lord. But only he fully knows our heart, our struggle, and our brokenness.

Only Jesus fully knows and embraces us.

That moment we experience God choosing us is the moment of conversion. In Jesus, the Father reaffirms his choice for humanity. Jesus embraces humanity in the Incarnation, and God and humanity are now forever united in communion. This choice for humanity isn't just about humanity in general; this is a choice for you. In his very nature, Jesus chooses you. This isn't just theology-speak. It's got to be personal. The moment of experiencing God choosing you is a profound moment of conversion. When I realized that I personally mattered to God, there was no going back. It was too personal. How could I walk away from someone who knew everything about me and loved me and called me? I just can't.

You have been chosen. Jesus is calling you into this adventure of life in relationship with him. He has chosen you for a new and abundant life. Take Bartimaeus as an example and jump up and go to him. He's calling your name.

Questions

What defines you? How do you think God sees you?

Jesus continues to choose you even at your worst moment. What stirs in your heart when you pray about this?

When Jesus calls us, he calls us out of something into his light, healing, freedom, grace, and love. What is he calling you out of?

Metanoia Moment

Come, Holy Spirit.

God loves you and chooses you personally. He is calling you out of what binds you and into a fuller life with him. Take a moment to ask for the grace to come out of what is holding you back. Now, reflect on God's personal love for you. Read John 3:16 but substitute it with your own name: "For God so loved ___ that he gave his only-begotten Son, that ___ should not perish but have eternal life." Meditate on this for a while and ask to feel God's personal love for you.

CHAPTER 8

POWER OVER
THE EVIL ONE

Sometimes it's difficult to resist.

I smelled it as soon as I walked into the house. It was my mom's "wacky-chocolate" cake, and she had made it for my younger brother's birthday. As I walked through the kitchen, it caught my eye: so beautiful, rich, and decadent. I walked by knowing that nothing good would come from my stopping to admire. I had been in my room for only a few minutes before I heard my name. "Dave." I had heard that voice before and knew it was probably best to ignore it, but it became more persistent. She (the cake) was calling my name.

I figured it wouldn't do any harm to go have a quick look, so I journeyed back to the kitchen. My mom makes an amazing wacky-chocolate cake. It's a chocolate cake with a wacky good chocolate frosting, which I guess is where it got its name.

For a moment or two I just looked at it, then it occurred to me — certainly, there was no harm in just tasting the frosting. Had it stopped there, I would have been fine. But I didn't. With the precision of a neurosurgeon, I cut a small piece of cake out of the corner of the pan. The cake was as good as I had remembered it. I must admit, I hadn't totally thought it through, which is often the case when giving into temptation. I looked at the cake with a corner missing and was *pretty* sure my mom was going to notice and *certain* she would figure out who did it. Obviously, I did what anyone else would have done. I took a napkin from the table behind me and rolled it up and neatly placed it in the corner cake had occupied a few short seconds earlier. I then, with the artistry of Caravaggio, took a bit of the excess frosting and moved it around a bit to cover the napkin so no one would be the wiser.

We can laugh about it now.

Evil Origins

To be honest, when I was younger I didn't think too much about the Devil. I knew the Devil existed, but I didn't give him too much attention. I recall SNL's "Church Lady" skits and howling with laughter as she referenced the cause of our temptations: "Could it be … SATAN?!" There was also the fact that our high school mascot was the Demons. It didn't seem odd at the time that we were cheering for the Demons. It does now, though.

When we try to picture the Devil, I think we tend to imagine the mascot: a little red figure with pointy ears, a tail, and a pitchfork. He's silly, but he isn't scary.

But maybe the Devil likes it when we think he's funny. He prefers if we don't take him too seriously. In his famous book *The Screwtape Letters*, C.S. Lewis writes from the perspective of a demon who is giving advice on how to tempt a soul. He says, "If any faint suspicion of your [the demon's] existence begins to arise in his [the soul's] mind, suggest to him a picture of something in red tights, and persuade him that since he cannot believe in that — it is an old textbook method of confusing them

— he therefore cannot believe in you."*

Not taking the evil one seriously is a step we take in peril. We must take the Devil very seriously; Jesus certainly did. For many Catholics, this is an invitation to conversion, a deeper understanding and experience of the spiritual life. God is real and so is the evil one, and the more we understand this, the closer we come to Jesus.

We see images of the Devil at the very beginning of Scripture. In Genesis, he begins to show his hand on how he will engage us when he tempts Adam and Eve. Scripture says that the evil one is the "most cunning" (Gn 3:1, NABRE), and we tend to forget that. He is incredibly cunning, and he's focusing all that cunning on our destruction.

If we pay close attention to how the evil one tricks Adam and Eve, we can learn how he is going to come after us. One of the first things he does is to cause Adam and Eve to doubt God. He asks Eve, "Did God say … ?" (Gn 3:1). He does this with us all the time. He gets us to question God, to question his word, his love, and his providential care for us. If we begin to doubt God, then we look somewhere else for answers. Often this happens when the Scriptures or the Church ask something of us that is difficult, and the evil one encourages us to look for answers that might be easier. "The Church is so out of touch" is a common tactic of the Devil.

After the evil one undermines Eve's trust in God, he lies to her. He tells her, "You will not die" (Gn 3:4) if she eats the forbidden fruit. Once Eve (or you or I) begins to doubt God, an opening is created, and the Devil will take advantage of this and work to fill that void.

This passage in Genesis is instructive. It shows us how the evil one works. He is cunning. He lies. He manipulates. He causes us to doubt God's word, his care and goodness. It needs to be abso-

---

* C.S. Lewis, *The Screwtape Letters,* in *The Complete C. S. Lewis Signature Classics*, 179–296 (New York: HarperCollins, 2007), 203–204.

lutely and perfectly clear, the Devil has one objective, and it is the destruction of your soul. And after the Fall, humanity was trapped and powerless under the control of the evil one. We were filled with fear and bound by sin. We weren't living in the fullness of who God created us to be. The Devil had us trapped in a web of deceit, and we were powerless. But there would be one who would free us from his dominion. The *Catechism* says, "The reason the Son of God appeared was to destroy the works of the devil" (394). Jesus came to confront the evil one and break the bonds that held humanity.

Jesus vs. the Evil One

Jesus' mission is to destroy the works of the Devil, and he takes this work seriously. We see Jesus confront the evil one all throughout the Gospels.

There are at least twenty-five instances where Jesus confronts the evil one in the Gospels. In the beginning of Luke, after his baptism, Jesus is filled with the Holy Spirit, and the Spirit leads him into the desert to be tempted by the Devil (see Lk 4:1–13). The battle that takes place between Jesus and Satan in the desert is key for us. It seemed like the evil one had total power over the world and some would even say over God. Jesus defeating the evil one reminds us that God is stronger. His victory over the tempter in the desert anticipates his final victory over the evil one in the Passion (CCC 539). Jesus' confrontation with the Devil shows us that victory over evil and temptation is possible — we are in fact not powerless!

In John 10:10 Jesus explains the goal of the evil one: "to steal and kill and destroy." In John 8:44, Jesus calls the evil one "the father of lies" and says "there is no truth in him." Jesus' point is very important here. Satan wants us to be separated from Jesus; he seeks our eternal damnation. The evil one will use any tactic to cause this, and we ought to feel a holy fear when reflecting on this reality — not a fear that overwhelms us, but one that invites us to be attentive. With Christ we have power over the enemy; without him we will perish.

In the Gospel of Mark, Jesus encounters the Devil in Capernaum:

> And they went into Capernaum; and immediately on the sabbath he entered the synagogue and taught. And they were astonished at his teaching, for he taught them as one who had authority, and not as the scribes. And immediately there was in the synagogue a man with an unclean spirit; and he cried out, "What have you to do with us, Jesus of Nazareth? Have you come to destroy us? I know who you are, the Holy One of God." But Jesus rebuked him, saying, "Be silent, and come out of him!" And the unclean spirit, convulsing him and crying with a loud voice, came out of him. And they were all amazed, so that they questioned among themselves, saying, "What is this? A new teaching! With authority he commands even the unclean spirits, and they obey him." (1:21–27)

In the Scriptures it becomes evident that Jesus has power over the enemy. He spoke with authority, and the evil spirits were bound to obey him. I love the fact that he didn't use fancy, showy rituals, just the power of his word.

A Share in Christ's Power

Jesus does not leave us alone to fight the evil one.

"The seventy returned with joy, saying, 'Lord, even the demons are subject to us in your name!' And he said to them, 'I saw Satan fall like lightning from heaven. Behold, I have given you authority to tread upon serpents and scorpions, and over all the power of the enemy; and nothing shall hurt you'" (Lk 10:17–19).

I remember hearing a wonderful story about a little girl who was afraid of a monster she thought was living in her closet. One night she was praying her bedtime prayers with her dad, and she expressed her concerns about the monster. Her father comforted her and told her that if there was anything in her room that she did not want there, she could make it go away by the power of Jesus' name.

The next evening, the little girl's mom put her to bed well before the girl was ready. A moment later the mother exasperatedly tells her husband, "I don't know what you taught your daughter last night, but she just ordered me out of her room in the name and the power of Jesus."

The little girl is actually on the right track. We have been given power, not in ourselves, rather in him. And this distinction is very important.

When I was a young missionary with NET, I was praying with someone who had been involved in the occult. It was evident that some evil spirits had attached themselves to him, and he was struggling from the effects of this. I remember praying (very stupidly, mind you) and saying to the evil spirits, "Get out, I am not afraid of you." This was not wise.

At that moment I experienced a power of evil and darkness I had never experienced before. I felt in my bones the presence of evil, and it frightened me. Very quickly, someone much wiser than I intervened, and soon there was tremendous peace in the situation. What became evident to me was that this person only prayed in the name of Jesus, and immediately things changed. For me it was a great learning experience. While it is true I have power, it is not my power. It is not in our own name, but in the name of Jesus that we have power.

It is important that we claim the power we have as Christians. At your baptism, you were freed from the power of the evil one; he no longer has a claim on your soul. The Rite of Baptism makes this very clear: "Almighty and ever-living God, you sent your only Son into the world to cast out the power of Satan, spirit of evil, to rescue man from the kingdom of darkness, and bring him into the splendor of your kingdom of light. We pray for this child: set him (her) free from original sin, make him (her) a temple of your glory."

In one of the Eastern Catholic rites, a part of their baptismal rite has the members of the congregation, during the prayer of exorcism, turn to the west and symbolically spit on the Devil. It's a poignant image.

The World, the Flesh, and the Devil

While Satan is ultimately behind all that is evil, he gets a lot of help. Sometimes "the Devil made me do it" is true. But I think we also give him too much credit, or perhaps don't fully comprehend how he works and how he works in things all around us. The evil one is active and tempts us in three areas: the world, the flesh, and the Devil. Having a better understanding of where the temptation is coming from helps us know how to stay free and defeat the enemy.

The World — The evil one has power over the world. But it's probably a good idea to clarify what is meant by the "world." The world, meaning all of God's creation, is obviously a good thing. In Genesis, God looks at all that he has made and declares that it is very good (see Gn 1:31). And in the Gospel of John we read that God loved the world so much that he sent his Son to save us (Jn 3:16). And yet there are other places where Scripture addresses the world or "powers of the world." When Satan tempts Jesus in the Gospel of Luke, he offers him all the kingdoms of the world (Lk 4:5). He can do this because the evil one has some measure of power and control over the world. The evil one can influence communal and social structures. The *Catechism* tells us, "The consequences of original sin and of all men's personal sins put the world as a whole in the sinful condition aptly described in St.

John's expression, 'the sin of the world'" (408). Sin has made the world into a place full of temptation.

We can see the influences of the enemy in a world where:

- money, convenience, lifestyles, and things are more important than people,
- the human body is something to be used and objectified,
- human sexuality is solely for pleasure, and gender is self-determined,
- government policies and social norms break down, attack, and minimize the traditional understanding of family with a father, mother, and children,
- greed consumes individuals, companies, and countries where little or no thought is given to those less fortunate, and
- truth and freedom are seen as subjective, human constructs not rooted in God.

Obviously, this list is not all inclusive. I'm only attempting to help us see the powers that are impacting the world. Unfortunately, they are powers of which we are often unaware. Saint Paul puts it so well: "The god of this world has blinded the minds of the unbelievers, to keep them from seeing the light of the gospel of the glory of Christ, who is the likeness of God" (2 Cor 4:4). We read also about "the dominion of darkness" (Col 1:13) and the perils of "following the course of this world" (Eph 2:2). Saint Paul is trying to express the underlying power and influence of the evil one on the world. It is imperative that we Christians not be blind or unaware of these influences, lest we fall prey to the tactics of the evil one.

The Flesh — The evil one can also influence our "flesh" or our bodies. Because of the Fall, human beings have concupiscence, an inclination toward sin. We struggle to live a life of virtue and grace and are often drawn toward sin and away from union with God. We are still fundamentally good. We are not defeated, but we are wounded.

We have a tension within us between the things of the flesh and the things of God. We all experience this tension but too often fail to recognize it, or if we do notice it, we don't have the grace to overcome it. The classic illustration of this is the all too popular person with an angel on one shoulder and a demon on the other. The reason that this image is used so frequently is that it resonates with us. We often experience this exact thing: We are tempted to do or moved not to do something, and we have an internal struggle. This is our battle with the flesh. Again, Saint Paul speaks so clearly to this in Galatians: "For the desires of the flesh are against the Spirit, and the desires of the Spirit are against the flesh; for these are opposed to each other, to prevent you from doing what you would" (Gal 5:17). The more we can become in tune with the ways of God's Spirit, the more we recognize the way the flesh draws us away from God. This can be through laziness, gluttony, lust, or any other sin of the flesh.

It sounds odd, but we need to become more familiar with the way the evil one speaks in his attempts to influence us. Jesus calls the Devil the father of lies (see Jn 8:44), and our understanding of this truth helps us in our battle with the flesh. What are the lies the evil one continually whispers in your ear that cause you to choose things that are not of God? They will sound different for everyone, but here are a few classic lies:

- "It's not that bad."
- "Everyone else is doing it."
- "I deserve this."
- "Compared to what my friend/sister/colleague does, this is nothing."

- "This won't hurt anyone."
- "No one needs to know about this."
- "I need this."

If we know how the evil one is going to attack us, we have a better chance of overcoming his temptations in the first place. This is why it's important that we become familiar with the word of God and that we spend time in prayer. Our minds and hearts need to be saturated with the things of God. When we hear the Devil say we are not good enough, we need to hear the Lord speak louder that we are wonderfully made. When Satan reminds us of sins of the past, God's word reminds us that we are forgiven. We must strive to be rooted in the truth that sets us free.

And while the stakes in this battle are huge, we don't have to be afraid or discouraged. When we are tempted, God can intervene; he really can — and will — help us. This isn't just wishful thinking but can and should be our lived reality. At the moment of being torn, tested, and tempted, we can call on the Lord for help. Sometimes this means we need to pray and walk away from a particular situation until we have more peace, or the anger subsides. This gives us a chance to take hold of the authority that was given to each of us at baptism.

We can work together with God to overcome temptation in our lives. We should strive to get into the habit of asking God for help. We can call on him when we're grouchy or tired and we know we're in danger of temptation. The key is to remember that we can't do this by ourselves.

The Devil — The Devil is a reality. The *Catechism* says, "Evil is not an abstraction, but refers to a person, Satan, the Evil One, the angel who opposes God. The devil is the one who 'throws himself across' God's plan and his work of salvation accomplished in Christ" (2851). The Devil is real, and his plan is to undermine God's plan. He wants to undo God's perfect design for your life and replace it with his own.

The Devil is behind all evil. He is "a murderer from the beginning" (CCC 2852). He seeks to kill and destroy our spiritual lives and union with God. He is "a liar and the father of lies," who causes us to doubt the Lord's promises. He is "the deceiver of the whole world." He is the accuser who causes us to define ourselves by our sin and brokenness rather than by God's grace and love. He is the divider who seeks to separate the people of God from one another, from the Church, and from God himself. This is where the Devil wants to most attack us. If he can divide the Church, the Body of Christ, then he can tear apart anything. It breaks my heart how divided we as Catholic Christians have become. We argue and fight over things that are supposed to give witness to our unity. We are supposed to be most united at Mass, and tragically it is when we are most divided. We become divided over the type of music, the songs, how one receives Communion, the types of vestments, who serves, who reads, and the list goes on. Clearly, we are going to have preferences on many of these things, but too many people allow the evil one to enter the dialogue and move us to demonize those we disagree with, and thus the Body of Christ becomes more fractured.

We open ourselves up to attack by the Devil by not living a life of virtue. In other words, the surest and most effective way to be attacked by the Devil is indulging in immoral behavior. In Galatians 5:19–20, Saint Paul gives us a pretty good list of vices that work against the Spirit of God, including spirits of anger, lust, greed, fear, gossip, drunkenness, and many other vices. If we want to experience freedom from the evil in our life, we need to strive to be certain that we are not opening doors that let the evil one in. Immoral or sinful behavior does just that: it opens the door wide to let the evil one have access to our heart. This door must be closed. Christ is always inviting us to a deeper conversion where the doors to sin are closed and sealed.

Victory

But how do we practically avoid being in bondage to the evil one? How do we avoid temptation and instead experience the fullness and freedom of life in Christ?

First, it is important to remember that the evil one does not have to have control over you. Yes, he's fighting for control, but he doesn't just have it. You have the power to give the enemy control, and you have the power to keep him from ever having control. You are in Christ and are a new creation (see 2 Cor 5:17), and greater is he that is in you than he that is in the world (1 Jn 4:4). We are invited to stand on this truth and live in God's freedom.

Pray to become more aware of yourself and the spiritual world. When and where are you most likely to be tempted? If you don't know the answers to these questions, you need to find them. If you do stupid, sinful things after the second beer, then don't drink a second beer. If there are certain movies or TV shows that you watch that you know are going to lead to trouble, then don't watch them. If there are people who are going to lead you to sin, then either stay away from them or learn to mitigate the impact they have on your life. If you are grouchy or impatient because you are always tired, work at getting more rest. The more we become aware of how we react in certain situations, the more likely we are to be able to cooperate with God's grace that is available to us.

Finally, it is important to always be aware that when we are in difficult moments — whether at home, work, or school — God is present. The Holy Spirit is alive and active in our lives and wants to be more present to us to help us overcome sin and bondage. Call on him, don't fight this battle alone. Call on the name of Jesus; he is present to us, and he is always giving us the grace we need for every moment. At the moment of difficulty or temptation, try to take a breath and ask for God's help. "Lord, I want to be patient! Help me at this very moment." I am amazed at the times when I intentionally stop and pray, how I handle situations with greater love and faithfulness. It's not like a magic pill, but the more I seek God's help, the more victory I experience.

Also be sure to call on Our Lady who crushes the head of Satan. Her intercession is powerful and necessary in this fight. The sacramentals of the Church, such as Rosaries, holy water, and icons, all help us in our battle against evil. In those moments when you are most tempted, there is always grace available. Christ gives us grace in the moment so that the evil one has no hold on us. Also, let's not forget that Saint Joseph is known as "the terror of demons" and there is power in seeking his intercession and protection.

The Power of the Resurrection

Finally, the greatest power of the evil one was always death. There was such a finality to it, such a loss. The Devil danced as Jesus' body was taken down from the cross and laid in the cold tomb. But it was a short dance.

Early in the morning of the third day, Mary Magdalene went to the tomb and learned that Jesus had risen. Peter and John would soon run to the tomb, and they too would discover that Christ was alive.

Jesus was risen. Death was defeated.

The Resurrection was Jesus' final victory over the evil one. Satan's final clutches are broken. The Resurrection brings the promise of victory for each of us. We run the race and fight the good fight. We struggle and persevere with Jesus at our side. We can claim the power and victory that is ours in Christ Jesus.

If Jesus can break the power of death, the ultimate power of the evil one, he can absolutely break the chains of your own struggles. He can break you out of anger, fear, shame, or whatever binds you. The evil one does battle against you, but it is a losing battle. It may be that at times we get knocked down, but the Lord will always help us get back up if we ask him. It's something that I know about all the saints: They all fell but kept getting up. God provides us all we need to live a dynamic life of faith, and I am confident that the Lord will provide you all you need to be a faithful son or daughter. Trust that the Lord has won the victory.

Questions

God is bigger than the powers of this world. How have you experienced this?

How have you experienced God's intervention when you were being tempted?

How do you see the powers of the world at work trying to seduce us?

Metanoia Moment

Come, Holy Spirit.

Saint Michael the Archangel, defend us in battle, be our protection against the wickedness and snares of the Devil. May God rebuke him we humbly pray; and do thou, O Prince of the heavenly host, by the power of God, cast into hell Satan and all the evil spirits who prowl about the world seeking the ruin of souls. Amen.

CHAPTER 9
THIS TEACHING IS HARD

I love the scene in *The Silver Chair*, part of the Chronicles of Narnia series, where Jill, dying of thirst, comes to a stream and to her surprise meets Aslan there. Aslan invites her to drink, but she is frightened and wonders if perhaps he wouldn't mind leaving. The softest of growls makes it clear that he is not going anywhere:

> "Will you promise not to — do anything to me, if I do come?" said Jill.
>
> "I make no promise," said the Lion.
>
> Jill was so thirsty now that, without noticing it, she had come a step nearer.
>
> "*Do* you eat girls?" she said.
>
> "I have swallowed up girls and boys, women and men, kings and emperors, cities and realms," said the Lion. It didn't say this as if it were boasting, nor as if it were sorry, nor as if it were angry. It just said it.

"I daren't come and drink," said Jill.

"Then you will die of thirst," said the Lion.

"Oh dear!" said Jill, coming another step nearer. "I suppose I must go and look for another stream then."

"There is no other stream," said the Lion.*

Jill eventually drinks from the stream under the care of Aslan, who is good and very, very strong. I believe this is an image of Jesus that would be good to focus on; I really dislike images of Jesus that make him look weak, wishy-washy, or like a '60s-loving hippie.

I think that's why I love the character of Aslan. He is strong, wild, fierce, protective, and good.

In the Basilica of the Immaculate Conception in Washington, DC, there is a large mosaic of Christ in Majesty. The image, above and behind the main altar, is a massive and imposing feature. In it, Christ sits in judgment. His face looks serious, stern, some say a bit angry. His arms are raised up and he is powerful. I heard an explanation one time that, in arguably the most powerful city in the world, you want to have an image of Christ equally powerful. Some people don't care for the mosaic; they say he is too imposing or intimidating. I like it. To me, it shows a Jesus who is powerful — he means business.

Of course, Jesus is loving, kind, and gentle. He is also strong, firm, intense, and focused. Jesus' teachings are so much more than syrupy-sweet tidbits that look nice on Pinterest. Take a moment and think about this. The things Jesus said and did bothered, angered, challenged, and frustrated so many people that they ultimately orchestrated having him killed. But all too often in our attempt to sanitize the teachings of Jesus and make them more palatable, we don't represent what he says.

---

* C.S. Lewis, *The Chronicles of Narnia Vol. IV: The Silver Chair* (Hong Kong: Enrich Spot, 2016), 15–16.

This Is Hard

One time I was having a conversation with a college student who was struggling with one of the teachings of the Church. The topic was causing him a lot of mental and spiritual anguish, and I could tell it was hard on him. After we had been talking for a while, he finally burst out, "Father Dave, Jesus wouldn't want this to be so hard!"

I want to tread lightly here. This young man's experience is sacred and intimate and his frustration so profoundly real. But his sentiment reveals, I believe, a deep-seated attitude that many people have. It illuminates an area where many of us need conversion. The young man expressed a sentiment that many people believe: that Jesus wouldn't ask things of us that are incredibly difficult, and that obedience shouldn't come with great cost.

We must confront this head on. Many of Jesus' teachings are very difficult and, on the surface, seem impossible, harsh, or unreasonable. There are some things Jesus said that we pay more attention to than others. We focus on the Jesus we like and avoid thinking about the Jesus who makes us uncomfortable. We love and memorize Scripture verses like "Judge not, that you be not judged" (Mt 7:1) and "God so loved the world" (Jn 3:16).

We love the words that make us feel good and affirm how we want to live. We like feeling safe and comfortable with Jesus. Those desires are good in and of themselves, but there is a danger to making Jesus into a person who never really says anything too challenging. We tend to conveniently forget that Jesus said some things that are profoundly difficult. Some of his words can make us uncomfortable, angry, frustrated, and even offended.

Woe, Woe, Woe!

Everything Jesus said was always ordered to our good. He always speaks out of love, even when his words seem perhaps … severe.

We can see this in one exchange between Jesus and the Pharisees: "Woe to you, scribes and Pharisees, hypocrites! For you are like whitewashed tombs, which outwardly appear beautiful, but within they are full of dead men's bones and all uncleanness. So you also outwardly appear righteous to men, but within you are full of hypocrisy and iniquity. You serpents, you brood of vipers, how are you to escape being sentenced to hell?" (Mt 23:27–28, 33).

Keep in mind that the scribes and Pharisees were trying to do the right thing. Of all the Jews, they were among the ones who were trying to be faithful and devout. Yet, something significant must change in their life, and Jesus does not hold back for fear of being too hard on them. Jesus desires their salvation and will say whatever is going to help bring that about.

But Jesus isn't done yet; it gets even better. When one of the scholars of the law hears what Jesus has to say, he approaches him and objects, "Teacher, in saying this you reproach us also." Bad idea. Jesus responds, "Woe to you lawyers also! For you load men with burdens hard to bear, and you yourselves do not touch the burdens with one of your fingers" (Lk 11:45–46).

Or in another place after Jesus was particularly firm on the Pharisees, his disciples approached him and asked, "Do you know that the Pharisees were offended when they heard this saying?" (Mt 15:12). Jesus replies, "Every plant which my heavenly Father has not planted will be rooted up. Let them alone; they are blind guides. And if a blind man leads a blind man, both will fall into a pit" (Mt 15:13–14). Like it or not, some things Jesus said are offensive to some people.

We live in a world where the unforgivable sin is to say something offensive. Lord have mercy if anyone is ever offended. In this context some attempt to portray Jesus as someone who would **never** say anything that one might find offensive. This is a serious problem for them, because much of what Jesus says ought to offend them.

Jesus never said he would not offend us, but he did say he was the Truth. He came to speak truth — even hard truth — into our lives.

I Can't Hear You!

I suppose it's human nature, but we tend to listen more to the things we like or the things we want to hear. We've all heard the phrase "selective hearing." My nieces and nephews never hear when they're asked to clean their rooms, but their ears miraculously open when their mom asks if they want a snack.

I think maybe we do the same thing with Jesus. We hear what we want and ignore what we don't. And often if we don't have a relationship with Jesus, if we are not living in his truth, his words are going to offend us. This is the case because we live in a world where many people believe that the individual determines what is true. "What's true for you is true, and what's true for me is true." We hear statements like "your truth" and "own your truth," but this is often in direct conflict with the words of Christ. This is part of the reason disagreements are volatile. If an individual believes he or she is the source of truth, the individual becomes defensive when confronted with the truth of Jesus. When you challenge someone's version of truth, you are challenging them, and this is met with great resistance.

When Jesus speaks truth — *and he always speaks truth* — it can be jarring. It convicts people who are outside of the truth. We have all had times where, for one reason or another, we don't want to hear the difficult word Jesus may be speaking into our lives and we are offended. It makes us uncomfortable, sometimes angry. If I believe I have the right to hate my neighbor because he has been such a jerk, and I hear Jesus say that I must love him and forgive him, if I am not open to conversion, to the truth of Jesus' words, then I will look for reasons why I don't have to forgive. I will listen to other people who have the same feeling toward my neighbor and will quickly feel justified in my hatred. At times, Jesus' words are very difficult. It was true during his earthly life, and it is true now.

The Hard Gospel

Jesus asks his followers to do hard things. Remember the story of the rich young man, when Jesus asks him to give up his possessions and follow him. The young man can't do that, so he walks away sad and despondent. This is important! For everyone who has ever said that Jesus wouldn't ask something so difficult, this story is illuminating. When it becomes clear to Jesus that what he is asking is difficult and it may be that the young man finds it too hard, Jesus doesn't give in. "Oh, I'm sorry! I didn't realize that would be so hard! You don't have to do that!" Jesus asks the young man to give up the thing that will keep him from eternal life. Jesus calls the young man to sacrifice and surrender, and it is difficult. Profoundly so.

The young man is free; he can come or go. Jesus doesn't force him, but rather he allows him to leave, even though he walks away sad. I can only imagine how this event must have broken Jesus' heart. He loved this young man, but he loved him and respected him too much to force him. "You want eternal life? OK, this is what YOU must do."

I can only imagine the young man going back to his friends. "He asked you to do what? Seriously? That's crazy. God wouldn't ask something so difficult." Or would he?

This Teaching Is Hard

In John's Gospel we hear another story where people quit following Jesus. In the Bread of Life Discourse in the sixth chapter of John, Jesus says, "Unless you eat the flesh of the Son of man and drink his blood, you have no life in you" (Jn 6:53).

We all know this story and how people were so troubled by what he said. It was too much for many of them; it was too hard (see Jn 6:60). This is the only place in the New Testament where people responded with "This is a hard saying," and many of them stopped following Jesus. And Jesus let them go.

I think this is key! Jesus lets them walk away. He knows this teaching is difficult — it was then and it still is today. There will never be a time when the teaching of the Eucharist isn't tough. But Jesus doesn't change or back down just because he realizes his words are difficult.

It's not like Jesus said, "OK guys, I know this is hard. So, you don't have to pay attention to it" or "Yeah, this is a tough one. How about you just pay attention to it for a little while, let's say 1,500 years or so. Then after that do what you want, believe what you want."

Just because something Jesus says is hard doesn't mean that his words need to change, or our interpretation of those words needs to change.

It can be tempting to respond, as many do, in this way: "This doesn't make sense, it's too hard. He must mean it's only a symbol."

No. Instead, we're the ones who need to change. We're the ones who need to be converted. Jesus' words and teachings are at times difficult and challenging, but they are always good and call us to deeper conversion.

Love Your Enemy

A lot of Jesus' most difficult teachings are the ones about how we relate to each other. We are all aware of the commandment to love our enemies. This wasn't merely a suggestion: "I say to you, Love your enemies, and pray for those who persecute you" (Mt 5:44). Who are your enemies?

I didn't think I had any enemies, until I asked the Lord who was my enemy. As I prayed, the Lord placed on my heart a woman who was the leader of a large organization that was responsible for a significant percentage of the abortions in America. I sensed the Lord asking me if I loved her. "I mean, I don't hate her."

It's not what he asked.

Do I love her? Love your enemies.

At that moment, I made the decision to pray for her. Not just a generic "Lord, bring an end to abortion," but I really prayed for her. Rosaries, holy hours, and fasting I offered for her. I prayed for her by name. I stalked her online a little bit and learned that she was married and had two children. I decided to send her a Christmas card, then an Easter card and let her know that I was praying for her and her family. I never heard back from her and didn't expect to, but something changed over time. This woman became a person to me, not an enemy. She loved her kids, wanted the best for them, worried about them, had hopes and dreams. In many ways very much like my own sister.

Over time, it became clearer to me that God doesn't have enemies. This woman is profoundly loved by the Father and is a daughter of God, and gradually my heart changed toward her. To be clear, I abhor the work that she does and what she stands for. But God did something in my heart for her, helping me to experience empathy and even sadness for her. This journey was a very transformative experience for me. It was a deep experience of conversion.

But that's not all. What about treating others the way that we would wish to be treated? We have heard this commandment our whole life, so it doesn't impact us like it did Jesus' listeners. Jesus puts a twist on a very common teaching. Other religions have something like this, but it is always in the negative. Their phrasing always includes some form of "do *not* do." Don't do to others what we don't want done to us. Do not cheat others, do not harm others, do not lie to others, et cetera. But Jesus tells us, "Whatever you would wish that men would do to you, do so to them" (Mt 7:12). We are called to something positive; Jesus totally raises the bar.

We aren't just called to avoid doing wrong, we are called to actively do good to others. If you love being affirmed, encouraged, and cared for, then you are commanded to do these things for others. Christian love is not passive, it is active and must be seen. Our life of faith must be lived in the world, and when we love, are patient, generous, and kind, we become the light that Jesus says we are.

Saint Francis was repulsed by lepers. There was perhaps the obvious reason that they had a disease, and he didn't want to become infected. But it was more than that: The leper represented everything that Saint Francis despised. They had no wealth, power, or influence. They lived in the valley with the outcasts, and Francis wanted nothing to do with them. At one point in his conversion, Francis was praying and heard the Lord say, "I can make what is bitter, sweet." Bitter? It was the lepers. "I can make what is bitter, sweet." Soon after this Francis was confronted by a leper. Francis embraced him, and Francis was changed. In this embrace he encountered Christ, and this changed him.

Why does the life of Francis radiate peace? Because he let God take what is bitter and make it sweet. God wants that same peace for you and me.

However, if we are honest with ourselves, I think sometimes we don't actually want to love others. I struggled with this when praying for the woman involved with abortions. I detest what she does and stands for, and I wasn't sure I wanted God to change my heart. It's not me with the problem, she's the one who needs to change. And then I remembered, "I can make that which is bitter, sweet."

Jesus calls us to embrace the leper, the enemy, the sinner, the antagonist, the sibling, the in-law, the coworker, the liberal, and the conservative, because they are important to him and loved by him. What will that look like for you?

Forgive ...

Peter asks Jesus how often we must forgive those who sin against us. Now, Peter goes out on a limb with an outrageous number, "How about seven times?" Jesus' reply to Peter is a little shocking. "I do not say to you seven times, but seventy times seven" (Mt 18:22). That's a lot of forgiveness. But there is more: If you fail to forgive others you will not be — can't be — forgiven (see Mt 6:15).

Forgiveness is hard, but we forgive because Jesus has forgiven us. Forgiveness isn't a feeling, it's a decision. If I only forgave when I felt like it, I would rarely forgive. We forgive one another because Jesus has forgiven us; we make the act of the will, we decide to forgive. Over time our heart will follow.

I recommend a little exercise for forgiveness. If you're struggling to forgive someone, take a moment and pray. Ask for the Holy Spirit to grant you the grace of forgiveness. Then, take a blank piece of paper and write on the top of the page: "[Insert name], I forgive you for ..." and then just write. Things will come to your mind that may not make sense, or that you don't think are a big deal. Don't worry, just write. Make an act of the will to forgive and let the Lord's mercy lead you. If you need a second piece of paper, or a third, or ... just keep writing as the Holy Spirit leads. When you are done, give the paper, the forgiveness, to the Lord and then destroy it. I guarantee in time, you will experience freedom and blessing from this.

Salvation

It's stunning how the world can totally twist what Jesus actually says and ends up presenting something completely opposite. There's a common belief in our culture that most people go to heaven. Hell — if people believe in it at all — is pretty much reserved for the mass murderers, rapists, and Hitler types. But this isn't what Jesus said. He told his followers, "Enter by the narrow gate; for the gate is wide and the way is easy, that leads to destruction, and those who enter by it are many. For the gate is narrow and the way is hard that leads to life, and those who find it are few" (Mt 7:13–14).

Most people hear exactly the opposite of what Jesus is saying. We want to believe that the road to heaven is wide and easy, and that most people choose it. But Jesus doesn't say that. The reality is that it is difficult. We must stay focused and constantly seek conversion. While of course it will be difficult, it is not overwhelming when we are living in the grace of Christ. In fact, quite the opposite: When we cooperate with God's grace, the burden is light.

Bear in mind that Jesus provides us with everything we could possibly need for this journey. This teaching ought not to cause fear in us. Recall that God's perfect love casts out all fear (see 1 Jn 4:18), and that God is for us (Rom 8:31), so we don't have to be overwhelmed. It should be sobering, but God is for us and is faithful. When we cooperate with him and his grace, we can be confident that we will inherit the kingdom of God. Here is a good way to discern the voice of God in our lives, as we try to follow him on the narrow way. If we feel discouragement, fear, or despair, this is not of God. On the other hand, if something stirs in our heart and we are awed, hopeful, and excited about how God is going to move in our life to bring about his plan, we can know that God is present.

Obedience

There's a famous story in my family about one of my nieces, Hannah. When she was little, my mom (her grandma) asked her to help her with something. Hannah got annoyed and exclaimed, "You're not the boss of me!" Well, Hannah's mom was listening in the other room. She called out "Hannah, EVERYONE is the boss of you." It's tough being a kid.

Obedience is difficult. Adam and Eve didn't like being told what to do, Hannah didn't, and neither do we. This speaks to the power of the flesh we spoke of earlier. We want to make our own rules and be our own bosses. We often don't want to do what he tells us to do. Which is one of the reasons I so appreciate that Jesus' first miracle was making wine for a party. I love the image of Jesus at a celebration like this, a party with his friends. He was probably laughing, snacking, and having a ball. But soon there is a major issue: The host runs out of wine. We know the story, but the miracle of the wine often gets all the attention, and Mary's instruction may get lost: "Do whatever he tells you" (Jn 2:5). This is essential for those of us who are trying to follow Jesus. We must do whatever he tells us. But we resist, we rebel against being told what we can and can't do.

This resistance and tension is a natural part of the process of ongoing conversion. We don't like being told what to do by Jesus, the Scriptures, the Church, the *Catechism*, our spouse, our friends, or our parents. But this is the point where conversion can take place. In conversion, we tell Jesus, "Not my will, but yours." That moment of surrender is a tremendous moment of grace. Bowing our head in obedience is transformative in our walk with Jesus.

Perhaps you're thinking, "I don't understand! It doesn't make sense. Why can't I? This isn't reasonable. It is so hard." I have heard all of this so many times. I'm sure I've said it many times. I get it, I really do, but there must be a point where we surrender, where we make an act of the will to be obedient. Saint Maximilian Kolbe said it this way: "In order that *obedience* be supernatural it must not proceed from reason, but from faith." This is metanoia, and obedience is essential.

The Gospel of Matthew offers a sobering picture of what metanoia really entails: "Not everyone who says to me, 'Lord, Lord,' shall enter the kingdom of heaven, but he who does the will of my Father who is in heaven. On that day many will say to me, 'Lord, Lord, did we not prophesy in your name, and cast out demons in your name, and do mighty works in your name?' And then I will declare to them, 'I never knew you; depart from me, you evildoers'" (Mt 7:21–23).

This is a hard passage because it shows us that it's not enough to just pray and talk about God. We also have to do what the Lord asks of us. Jesus made it clear that if we want to love him, we must keep his commandments (see Jn 14:15). He has given us the commandments for our good and for our protection. This doesn't mean we won't ever sin or that we will no longer need God's ever-new mercy. But we cannot simply dismiss Jesus' hard teachings and act like they don't matter.

We can take comfort in remembering that Jesus is not asking anything of us that he didn't do himself. He was obedient to the point of death. In the Garden of Gethsemane, he wrestled with the Father's will: "If it is possible, let this chalice pass from me" (Mt 26:39). Our salvation comes about through Jesus' obedience to his Father. We will also find salvation by being obedient to our heavenly Father.

Gifts for the Journey

Fun chapter, huh?

Everything in this chapter must be looked at through the lens that God is love. Everything Jesus said and the teaching of Saint Paul all unpack this fundamental reality. The purpose of Jesus' coming was to reveal the love of his Father and lead us home to our Father.

When we hear some of these teachings and it makes us uncomfortable, it is good to pray in that moment. We can call out to the Holy Spirit and say, "Move in my heart. I know this is about your love for me. Help me embrace this and see how it's about your love for me."

We can trust that Jesus won't ask anything of us that he won't provide for with the necessary graces. When he calls, he will give us the grace to answer. We can receive this grace through prayer, through Scripture, and through the sacraments. The Sacrament of Confession brings forgiveness for our sins and provides the grace to be faithful and sin no more. The Sacrament of Holy Communion strengthens us for the journey. He gives us the Holy Spirit to empower and help us. Jesus doesn't ask us to do heroic things without giving us tools and strength for the task.

One of my very favorite quotes is from the Office of Readings on the feast of Saint Joseph, which is celebrated on March 19. Saint Bernardine of Siena beautifully writes what I am trying to express: "There is a general rule concerning all special graces granted to any human being. Whenever the divine favor chooses someone to receive a special grace, or to accept a lofty vocation, God adorns the person chosen with all the gifts of the Spirit needed to fulfill the task at hand." The heavenly Father has called you to a lofty vocation, to be a disciple of Jesus. Do not be afraid; God is with you, and you will do well.

Questions

What are some of your favorite things that Jesus said, words that minister to your heart?

What is a word that you have struggled with? How do you wrestle with this?

What is bitter that you want God to make sweet?

What is an example of something that you once struggled with, but the Lord changed your heart?

Metanoia Moment

Come, Holy Spirit.

If there are any hard teachings that are causing you confusion or anxiety, ask Jesus to come and move in your heart. Ask him for conversion and conviction, but above all ask that you can know his deep love for you. Trust that he will always provide the necessary grace for you.

CHAPTER 10
DO YOU LOVE ME?

We need to know and be reminded often that we are loved. As kids, when I or one of my younger brothers got in trouble and were sent to our room, we would use the one who hadn't been incarcerated as a runner. The runner would take notes back and forth to Mom to get a sense of how long we would be stuck in our rooms. Generally, we had multiple choice questions, and Mom would usually play along. Eventually, one of the notes would be very simple:

Mom, I'm sorry. Do you still love me?
Circle one: Yes — No

When the messenger sibling came back from their mission, the note always had "yes" checked. There was never any doubt what her response would be, but it never hurt to be reminded.

This reminds me of the musical *Fiddler on the Roof.* In one of the more famous scenes, the main character, Tevye, asks his wife, Golde, if she loves him. Golde responds by listing all the things she has done for him. She's washed his clothes, cooked his food, cleaned his house, raised his children. Still Tevye asks if she loves him. The list is nice, but he wants to hear her say that she loves him. "After twenty-five years, it's nice to know," he famously says.

There is something so intimate and vulnerable about the question, "Do you love me?" The person asking is putting their heart out there in such an exposed manner. It's an all-or-nothing question with only one hoped-for answer.

We were created to love and to be loved. We long to be accepted wholly and entirely, to be seen, to enjoy intimacy, and to be understood.

While we want to ask, "Do you love me?" a part of us is terrified by what we might hear. That's why it's so striking when Jesus meets Peter on the shore of the Sea of Galilee and asks the question that burns in all our own hearts: "Do you love me?"

On the Shore

The Sea of Galilee is one of my favorite places on earth. Whenever I am there, I always go down to the shore to watch the sunrise. There are all kinds of questions when you are in the Holy Land about exactly what happened where. But there is absolute certainty that Jesus walked along the seashore. And John's Gospel says that he did this early in the morning as the sun was rising. It's so beautiful and calming to watch the early morning light change color and brighten as I listen to the waves lap gently on the shore and feel the sun slowly start to warm my face as it rises. There is such a peace, and it is simply graced.

That same sun rose over the same sea early one morning nearly two thousand years ago. And Peter was there to watch it, but he wasn't filled with peace — more like shame and probably regret. It was early in the morning after Jesus' resurrection, but before his ascension into heaven. Of course, Peter was overjoyed that Jesus had returned, but he still felt somewhat lost. I can't imagine the inner turmoil that Peter must have gone through during that time. He had walked away, even though he said he wouldn't, and acted like he didn't even know Jesus. Peter didn't know what to do with himself, so he did what he had always done in the mornings of his former life. He went fishing with some of the other disciples. They hadn't caught anything, as usual, and were coming back to shore. As the sun rose and the boat approached the shore, I imagine Peter was feeling tired and discouraged and still preoccupied.

They could see a man on the beach, and he instructed them to try casting their fishing nets on the other side of the boat. When they did, they caught so many fish that they weren't even able to pull the net back in. Peter, being Peter, jumped out of the boat and started swimming to the shore.

There he was, soaking wet and standing before Jesus, waiting for the others. What was going through his mind? I'm sure he had played the scene in his mind a million times. They really hadn't talked about it, and maybe a part of him wanted to, while another part never wanted to think about it again. For the first time since the Resurrection, he was alone with Jesus, and he had no clue what to say.

After they've finished eating, Jesus asks Peter the question he's been simultaneously hoping for and dreading.

"Peter, do you love me?"

I bet it broke his heart. It confirmed what he was afraid of, that Jesus didn't think Peter loved him. Of course, he did, but Jesus didn't know.

At the same time, Peter was probably dying to answer this question. He was so riddled with guilt that maybe this was the opportunity to make it right. He had another shot, another chance to prove to Jesus how much he really did love him.

The actual question asked is a bit more detailed. "Do you love me more than these?" (Jn 21:15). There are differing opinions on what Jesus means by "these." Some scholars say that Jesus may have been pointing to the fishing equipment, the boats, nets, lines, things like that. The things that marked his past life and career. Jesus is asking him, "Do you love me more than all of that, more than those things?"

Other scholars think that "these" refers to the other disciples. Did Peter love Jesus more than he loved his friends and fellow disciples? Did he love Jesus more than he valued the thoughts and opinions of others? Was he more concerned with pleasing his peers than pleasing Christ?

All of that is interesting and I suppose good for us to discern. They are good questions for us to ask ourselves. But I think the only thing Peter heard was, "Do you love me?"

"Yes, Lord; you know that I love you" (Jn 21:15).

There, he got to say it, he was able to tell Jesus that he loved him.

Again, Jesus asks Peter, "Do you love me?"

"Dang it, just what I thought, he doesn't believe me," thinks Peter. The first question was great, an opportunity for Peter to redeem himself. The second time confirms his fear: Jesus isn't sure of his love.

What a time of conversion this is for Peter. Jesus is giving him the opportunity to affirm his love, and each time he does this, he is liberated from his past. And if we think about it, this is such a beautiful, humble action of Jesus. The living God puts himself out there, makes himself vulnerable, and asks if we love him. Every time we profess our love for Jesus, it is a metanoia moment. It's another opportunity to say that we love.

As we all know, Jesus ultimately asks Peter this question three times. Each time Peter tells Jesus that he loves him, and I suppose that with each statement of love, Peter feels the shame of his denial decrease.

There will be a day when each of us will hear this same question from Jesus: "___, do you love me?" There are times I hope that

Jesus doesn't have to ask me this question. I hope that he would be able to tell by the way I've lived my life that I love him. But of course, Jesus will ask me this question the same way he asked Peter. Because ultimately this question isn't really for Jesus' benefit. It's for Peter; it's for me; it's for you. Jesus wants us to examine our hearts. He wants us to contemplate our love for him. He wants to provide us the opportunity to say, "Yes Lord, I love you."

Feeding the Sheep

There is a connection between this love and mission. Peter affirms his love for Jesus and is immediately given a mission. The love of Jesus invites us into his mission and the mission of the Church. When Peter responds that yes, he loves Jesus, he is immediately asked to tend the Lord's sheep. The love of God always has an outward thrust, sending us to share this love with others.

As Christians, you and I are called to participate in Jesus' mission. We are invited to help reveal the kingdom of God. The conversion we experience is never meant to be held to ourselves but needs to always be shared with others. Your story will impact someone else's life. We have experienced the love of Christ and are now called to share what we have heard and experienced with others. We are to be evangelists.

The moment that many people hear the word "evangelize," they check out. The idea of evangelizing can be intimidating, uncomfortable, and threatening. I've had many people tell me that they never realized they were called to be evangelists. But if you're baptized, you're called to be an evangelist. Tragically, we live in an age where Christians have done a terrible job giving witness to the goodness of Christ. More than ever we need men and women who live lives that testify to God's glory. This is at the heart of being who we are created to be. It is constitutive to being a Christian.

The first time I identified myself as an evangelist was in an emergency room waiting to have my appendix taken out. I was a twenty-one-year-old missionary with NET. One morning I wasn't feeling well and had a terrible stomachache, and over a few hours, the pain kept getting worse. (One time I made the mistake while giving a talk of saying it was like having a baby. I was surprised at the end of the talk at the line of women who wanted to chat. So, the pain was bad, but to be clear, it was *nothing* like having a baby.) I had a feeling that maybe it was my appendix and went to the ER to get it checked out. It was determined that it was indeed my appendix, and they were going to have to do surgery immediately. As they were prepping me for surgery, a lovely woman asked me all kinds of questions.

Full name?

Age?

Address?

Social Security number?

Medical history?

Parents' full names?

Favorite color?

Dogs or cats?

Weight?

I found myself getting a bit frustrated. Can't we deal with the questions later? I'm dying here.

Then she asked, "Occupation?" I paused and responded, "Evangelist."

"An evangelist? Really? That's wonderful. What exactly do you do?"

Again, I wasn't at my best and wanted to have my appendix removed from my body as soon as possible. So, I wasn't really up for small talk. I stated that I would love to talk more with her about this, but could we put it off till after the surgery. She said that would be fine.

"Do you have your insurance information handy?"

The thing is, being an evangelist really isn't an occupation as such, but is more just basic Christian living. To be an evangelist is to share the Gospel — which is Jesus — with others. Maybe this feels daunting, but we evangelize all the time for all kinds of things.

We are an evangelist for whatever we love. People evangelize for the latest diet fads, workout routines, sports teams, books, philosophies, hobbies, or political parties. When we find something we love, we want to share it with others. When we have good news, we want everyone to hear it.

It's the same with Christian evangelization. When we come to know the love of Christ, we are moved to share it with others. Look at what the *Catechism* says: "From this loving knowledge of Christ springs the desire to proclaim him, to 'evangelize,' and to lead others to the 'yes' of faith in Jesus Christ" (429). Our relationship with Christ will lead us into the work of evangelization.

Pope St. Paul VI talks more about this call to evangelization: "The person who has been evangelized goes on to evangelize others. Here lies the test of truth, the touchstone of evangelization: it is unthinkable that a person should accept the Word and give himself to the kingdom without becoming a person who bears witness to it and proclaims it in his turn."*

Evangelization is not just a good thing to do. It's not "extra credit" for the baptized. Evangelization is central to the converted Christian life. It ought to be unthinkable that we could have a life with Christ and not feel called to share it with others. Proclaiming the kingdom and the Gospel is not optional. It's actually a commandment. So many people need a change of heart in this area: It really is your job to share the good news of God's reign.

It's Your Turn

So, what is stopping you from answering the call to evangeliza-

---

* Paul VI, *Evangelii Nuntiandi*, par. 24, http://www.vatican.va.

tion? Is it fear of rejection? Fear is normal, but it shouldn't stop you. If we really love God "more than these," we don't have to be afraid of what "they" think.

Are you afraid because you feel like you lack knowledge or training? While there are things that we can learn that will help us to be more effective evangelists, what is more important is being aware of what God has done for you. How have you been converted? How has God changed your life? If you can answer these questions, then tell someone about it.

One of the best examples of the power of evangelization is the story of the woman at the well in the fourth chapter of John. In this story, a Samaritan woman has a powerful encounter with Jesus, and this encounter changes her. She must tell everyone what Jesus has done for her and runs back to her town proclaiming what God has done. As she tells her story and witnesses to her encounter with Jesus, many of the people in her town begin to believe in Jesus, too (see Jn 4:39). The woman wasn't well-trained, hadn't been through a workshop or attended a conference, but she encountered the love of God and just had to tell people.

Alex had a similar story. Twice a week he spent time ministering to and evangelizing teens. When I asked him why he did this, he stated, "Father Dave, I didn't encounter Jesus until I was forty years old. I made a promise that I would do all I could to make sure that others don't have to wait till they are forty to come to know Christ."

This is feeding the sheep.

In the end, evangelization is telling your story. What has God done for you? You don't have to wear a special tie with the image of the crucifixion on Good Friday, and you don't have to hand out Rosaries at the mall. You don't have to write books or speak to a large crowd. You don't need a blog or a podcast. If you're called by God to do those things, great. But the absolutely necessary part of evangelization is you living your life in a manner that is attractive to others and telling them what animates you. All you must do is give away what you received.

I once listened to an atheist who was talking about Christians and evangelization. He said, "If I believed the story of Jesus, I would tell everyone I knew all about it. If I believed it was true, I couldn't stay quiet."

I think this is the attitude we should have about evangelization. We know the truth of the Gospel, and we know Jesus in a personal way. We are converted. We are loved. He has done great things for us. Now we just need to be ready to tell others all about it. There's nothing stopping us. Not everyone is going to respond in the way we would like — in fact, many people won't listen. Some will ridicule and mock us, so let's not be surprised. It's not up to us how people respond or what is considered "success." Rather, what is asked of us is to see that there are men and women lost, sheep who are starving. We need to give them something to eat.

Questions

God is love and reveals to us what authentic love is. How is what the world offers as love different from the love of God?

The Lord has a mission for you. What is he asking of you?

Metanoia Moment

Come, Holy Spirit.

Take a moment to rest in the love of God. Know that at every moment of every day, God is beholding you with the greatest love. You are not alone. There are others who need to hear what you have heard and see what you have seen. Ask the Lord to place someone on your heart and reach out to them.

EPILOGUE

In the third chapter of the second letter of Peter we hear that God is patient with us so that we can come to *repentance*. The word Peter uses is *metanoia*. God is patient with us because he desires us to be with him forever. He generously gives us time and grace so that we are able to root out everything in our lives that is not of him.

God is patient with you, so please be patient with yourself.

Our journey of metanoia is a lifelong process. While we are alive, it's never finished. This ought not cause you stress or anxiety; rather, it should fill you with hope. True conversion, the type that is lasting, deep, and transformative, takes time. Every area of our life, mind, heart, and flesh should be open to conversion. It will take time and precision for our conversion to be complete.

Forgive the analogy, but it's like we are a block of precious marble. Being compared to a piece of rock may not move your heart, but stay with me. God continues forming us and chiseling away what is not of him. In order for the work to be completed and beautiful as intended by the artist, it will take time and meticulousness. Piece by piece the Lord will remove what is not of him.

In this book I have shared numerous ways the Lord has

worked in my heart. The Lord continues to shape my heart by showing me ways that I can love and be loved more perfectly. God molds my mind and my attitudes that need to change so that I can think more like him. Lies so easily get attached to my brain, and I am so grateful that the Lord continues to shine his light in my mind and remove what is not true. I know he is not done. There is more that needs to be transformed. I've also shared elements of the spiritual life in which I have come to a deeper understanding, but there is more to learn, and I know God wants me to gain deeper understanding of his mysteries.

Ultimately, we are invited to live our life continually open to conversion. There are times when you may get impatient and think you should be past something. You may think, "I shouldn't still be plagued by a certain sin, a question, doubt, or a shortcoming." Be at peace. Try not to stay there for long, but instead claim the truth that the Lord is patient with you. Even your present struggle is an invitation to a deeper relationship with Jesus.

I've found that working toward an eternal perspective helps. God always has been and always will be patient, so you can be as well. To be honest, I find the fact that the Lord is always at work in my life to be exciting. I look forward to seeing what he reveals, what deeper insight the Lord wants to show me next.

What's next — what does he have in store for you? Take a moment and pray that you would know Jesus for exactly who he is, and if there is something that needs to be converted, some metanoia still necessary, give God the time to bring about this change in your mind and heart.

If you don't see yourself as God sees you, seek the Lord's grace and be purified.

If you don't love your enemy, your neighbor, your brother the way Jesus does, then ask the Lord to bring metanoia. Pray for the desire to live in the absolute truth of who you are, who your neighbor is, and who God is.

This is the desire of my heart: to live Christ. I know the space between my desire and reality is vast, but Jesus delights in my desire to be more like him and will never give up on me.

He will always accept me as I come to him, and he will also continue to invite me to a fuller, more abundant life. I hear his words in the depths of my being: The kingdom of God is at hand. I want to be a part of the kingdom that Jesus established. I want to be liberated from the kingdom of the world and live for him and his kingdom alone. For this to move from desire to reality, it is essential that I metanoia. May it be so.

ACKNOWLEDGMENTS

Thank you, Lord, for never giving up on me.

Also, great thanks to Kaitlin Rooney who helped me organize my thoughts and get them to paper. And a special thank you to Niki Kalpakgian for knowing my voice.

ABOUT THE AUTHOR

Fr. Dave Pivonka, TOR, is the president of Franciscan University of Steubenville. For more than thirty years Father Dave has journeyed with men and women in their walk of faith by providing spiritual direction and retreats and leading pilgrimages. He is a well-known author, conference speaker, and creator of the powerful video series *Metanoia* and *The Wild Goose.*